Anxiety

in

Relationship

for Couples

The Secrets to Feeling More Confident and Secure in Your Relationship by Managing Jealousy, Negative Thinking, Fear of Abandonment, Insecurity, and Attachment Issues

© Copyright by **Rose R. Murphy**

Rose R. Murphy

The content contained within this book may not be reproduced, duplicated or transmitted without direct written permission from the author or the publisher.

Under no circumstances will any blame or legal responsibility be held against the publisher, or author, for any damages, reparation, or monetary loss due to the information contained within this book. Either directly or indirectly.

Legal Notice:

This book is copyright protected. This book is only for personal use. You cannot amend, distribute, sell, use, quote or paraphrase any part, or the content within this book, without the consent of the author or publisher.

Disclaimer Notice:

Please note the information contained within this document is for educational and entertainment purposes only. All effort has been executed to present accurate, up to date, and reliable, complete information. No warranties of any kind are declared or implied. Readers acknowledge that the author is not engaging in the rendering of legal, financial, medical or professional advice. The content within this book has been derived from various sources. Please consult a licensed professional before attempting any techniques outlined in this book.

By reading this document, the reader agrees that under no circumstances is the author responsible for any losses, direct or indirect, which are incurred as a result of the use of information contained within this document, including, but not limited to, errors, omissions, or inaccuracies.

Table of Contents

Rose R. Murphy

INTRODUCTION

Anxiety is an emotional state, pleasant or unpleasant, associated with a condition of alertness and fear towards everything outside; generally it is an "exaggerated" reaction to the real situation. This emotional state involves not only the individual, but also the people around him/her.

The symptoms of this emotional state are nervousness, apprehension, insomnia, sleeplessness, apnea, easy crying, palpitations, weakness and stomach cramps.

According to the great psychoanalyst S. Freud at the origin of the appearance of anxiety there are tensions or "battles" within the individual that have not been resolved. Generally all individuals experience feelings of anxiety, which - if properly motivated - remains a transient sensation with a positive effect; conversely, anxiety episodes that arise without real justification due to incomprehensible and non-emotional reasons, are at the origin of excessive reactions characterizing the pathological or negative anxiety. In most cases the pathological anxiety is accompanied by "panic attacks", acute crises characterized by fear, palpitations and disorderly and aphinalistic behaviors. The so-called "phobias" are instead attituding of real but not objective fear for contextual situations, or animals or objects. The treatment of anxiety includes:

Pharmacological treatments for established diseases, when the anxiety is due to an organic disease.

In case of "situational anxiety" it is necessary for the individual to overcome that difficult moment by himself, possibly he can use hypnotic-sedative drugs for short periods.

In case of "chronic anxiety", long-term drug therapy with hypnotic-sedative drugs, possibly combined with psychotherapy.

In this book we will deal with anxiety in relationships, how to overcome anxiety, jealousy, negative thinking, manage insecurity and attachment. Learn how to eliminate couple conflicts to establish better relationships.

Enjoy reading!

CHAPTER 1   • What is Anxiety in People

It's easy to say anxiety. This condition, which is now considered almost an obligatory appendix to the stressful life of today's society, is actually very complex and multifaceted.

Meanwhile, it is necessary to specify that it is a set of cognitive, behavioral and physiological reactions, which does not always give rise to the same type of disorders.

Then, we should not forget that basically anxiety is not an abnormal manifestation. It is a common emotion, which is part of the legacy of human evolution. In fact, anxiety is an emotion that is activated when we are faced with a situation that we subjectively perceive as dangerous.

It becomes a problem when it begins to manifest itself in a very excessive way, or particularly frequently, to the point of becoming chronic. At these levels, anxiety can have a substantial impact on people's normal activities, preventing them from leading a peaceful life.

In these cases we speak of an anxiety disorder that, depending on the different situations, requires specific and targeted treatments.

What is Anxiety?

With this definition of anxiety, it is intended to describe a situation in which we are afraid, but we do not know what we are afraid of.

In anxiety we are afraid of a danger or a negative future event, but these are not clearly outlined. It is precisely this characteristic that distinguishes anxiety from fear, which instead has a clear and defined object. In anxiety we live a widespread state of alert, as if we were constantly in a state of fear, but without knowing clearly what is the object of our fear.

Let's make some examples to better clarify the concept, which will also help us to distinguish the physiological anxiety from the pathological one.

Physiological anxiety

Anxiety can be defined as physiological when it has an adaptive function for people. This means that physiological anxiety has characteristics that help people to survive and adapt better to their environment. In this sense, anxiety is linked to the mental construction of a pattern of anticipation: I am anxious because this serves to assess the danger/risk.

An example of physiological anxiety is the one we feel when we have to do an examination. It is adaptive, because if students were not afraid to take an exam, perhaps they would not study enough and would not pass it. So a bit of anxiety can help to prepare for it.

In this case we talk about anxiety, and not fear, because in an exam there is no certain outcome: if we were in front of a lion, the danger would be real, and the outcome quite sure, so we could talk about fear. But in the exam, if we have studied and are sufficiently prepared, what could happen so bad that we are afraid? We could fail and repeat the exam: what is so scary about that?

Actually, in this case what we feel is a state of anxiety due to the fear of an external evaluation: the result of the exam is not all in our hands but depends on how the professor will evaluate us. In fact, in this outcome, there are a series of expectations and evaluations on ourselves, so the anxiety is more related to a fear on the self-image.

Pathological Anxiety

If this state of anxiety for the examination becomes such that we are unable to present ourselves for the examination, we can speak of pathological anxiety and anxiety disorder.

So the anxiety becomes pathological when it prevents us from living normal daily activities, such as having social relationships, working, having emotional relationships, etc. Returning to the example of the exam, if the anxiety is so strong that we do not graduate for fear of taking the exam, we speak of pathological anxiety: it becomes a disorder that takes away our ability to assert ourselves professionally, to have an autonomous life and so on.

Sudden anxiety and state anxiety

We must mention a further distinction between state anxiety and sudden anxiety.

State anxiety is a transient condition, which is activated only to respond to specific situations. It may go so far as to be pathological, but its characteristic remains that it is always activated only in response to certain situations, which the person considers dangerous.

Sudden anxiety refers to a general disposition towards anxiety, so people respond with anxiety to all situations that contain a danger, objective or subjective. The term 'trait' is used precisely to indicate an emotional tendency to worry and scare in a systematic way. The presence of trait anxiety can be a sign of the presence of pathological anxiety.

Difference between anxiety and fear: distinguish them and understand their value

Anxiety is different from fear, since fear is a functional reaction to face an immediate danger while anxiety aims to address a concern about the verifiability of a future event. Psychologists emphasize this aspect of "immediacy" typical of fear, in contrast to the act of "prediction" that characterizes anxiety. It should be stressed that anxiety and fear are not necessarily "bad" feelings, but on the contrary have an adaptive role. Fear, in fact, is fundamental in the "attack or escape" response, which allows us to mobilize all our resources to face the threat or, alternatively, escape from it. For this reason in the right circumstances a reaction of fear can save our lives. In the same way, anxiety helps us to identify future threats and to guard against them, designing hypothetical scenarios in which we could be involved and, in that case, we should face the feared situation. In fact, as Yerkes and Dodson's law (1908) teaches us, a right degree of anxiety (therefore not excessive) allows us to be more efficient than when we are calm. However, in humans, but also in animals, anxiety often goes beyond its adaptive aspects, i.e. useful, to other non-adaptive aspects, as anxious reactions are generalized to a series of 'neutral' situations.

Features and Components of Anxiety

What comes into play when anxiety sets in? The perception of a danger.

This perception has a neurophysiological component and a component of thought representation.

To explain the concept in simple terms, we can say that the neurophysiological perception of a danger occurs according to this scheme:

- Thought: I see a lion and think that I am in danger.
- Feeling: I feel the emotion of fear. Emotions are a synaptic circuit: they are felt because in the body neurons are activated in a certain way. The pupils of the eyes dilate, the hair stands up on the head, the hair on the arms rises, blood pressure increases and also the heartbeat: the nervous system prepares itself for danger.
- Behaviour: I feel fear and run away.

Anxiety and environment

Our anxious and fearful reaction can be genetically determined, but it is also linked to the representation of thought. If, for me, finding myself in front of a lion is a normal thing because my parents were circus tamers, this condition will not represent a danger. If, on the other hand, as a child I was excessively subjected to a climate of fear, and I had a very anxious mother or father, some of my synaptic circuits remain more easily activated in this sense. Therefore, I will more easily enter a state of anxiety.

According to research, anxiety can be learned from the environment: it depends on what we learned in our childhood.

Our reality is always a representation. Although it is an objective given, it is always constructed through the senses, therefore through our ability to imagine. So, when we perceive stimuli, if we have learned that these stimuli are a source of danger, we automatically associate them with an anxiety response. If my mom in general is anxious when faced with new things, I probably get anxious too when I have new things to do. Also, another important aspect to consider is that, usually, when the person who is structurally anxious thinks he can't face new things, this anxiety depends a lot on his idea about himself. He does not feel capable, feeling incapable he gets scared and therefore feels anxiety.

Causes: hereditary, biological and unconscious factors

The causes of anxiety are different and complex. Wanting to make a synthesis, we can divide into 3 macro categories the factors that determine states of anxiety more or less serious:

- The hereditary factors. There are genetic studies that have found that, frequently, individuals with anxiety disorders have a family member suffering from the same pathology.
- The biological factors. According to research carried out on the human brain, anxiety could be caused by alterations in the amount of certain neurotransmitters. Therefore, the biological site of anxiety seems to be the Locus Coeuruleus, which is responsible for activating or deactivating the inhibitory neurons that are activated by gamma-Amino Butyric Acid (GABA).
- The unconscious factors. According to Freud's theory, anxiety is caused by unconscious conflict.

Freud's unconscious factors

For Freud, anxiety is therefore linked to an intrapsychic aspect, and has two meanings:

- It is the manifestation of a neurotic conflict, that is, a struggle between a desire (sexual or aggressive) and the prohibition of the superego, aimed at inhibiting the awareness of desire, because it is considered reprehensible.
- It is the way to remove the awareness of the conflict itself.

So we, not being able to get in touch with these unacceptable desires, we experience anxiety, as a sign of danger of emergence of those contents that we want to remove. The person feels anxiety, but does not know why: to remove it, he should decode his experience and understand what is frightening him.

Other Causes of Anxiety

Then there can be existential anxieties, which give rise to anxiety, for example with respect to evolutionary phases, such as: I am retiring and I feel anxiety about the future.

As Fromm said, anxiety expresses the distance of contemporary man from himself, that is, from the fundamental values and needs of human beings, such as having meaningful emotional relationships and expressing themselves in their social context.

In fact, widespread is the anxiety derived from a deficient inner secure base.

When people have not been able to build in their mind the experience of the safe base, introducing in their mind the experience of an adult, usually a parent, who takes care of them and is able to tune in with their emotional needs, often manifest anxiety disorders. In fact, when the child experiences a 'caregiver' that offers security, he gradually stores within himself this supportive, comforting and generally positive relationship, bringing it back into his adult life. On the other hand, when this feeling full of security is missing, anxiety is one of the basic signs related to this situation of generalized insecurity.

So, to summarize, anxiety related to intrapsychic factors may be related to:

- internal impulses, according to Freud's theory;
- existential anxieties;
- lack of a secure internalized basis.

CHAPTER 2 • Categories of Anxiety Disorders

Below are some of the most common anxiety disorders.

Specific and Social Phobia

The specific phobia is characterized by a marked and persistent fear, excessive or unreasonable, caused by the presence or waiting for a specific object or situation (e.g. airplane, enclosed spaces, spiders, dogs, cats, insects, etc.). Specific phobias are therefore behaviors of avoiding specific things or situations, which activate a disproportionate and unreasonable anxiety.

Social phobia is characterized by a marked and persistent fear of social situations or benefits that involve exposure to unfamiliar people or the possible judgment of others. In such situations, the person fears showing anxiety or acting humiliatingly and embarrassingly.

Even a certain degree of social anxiety can be seen as a common experience when, for example, speaking in public, taking an exam, or attending parties or meetings without knowing anyone. The boundary between normality and pathology can be seen in the strong discomfort and the considerable impairment of social and working life that the disorder produces in people who suffer from it.

Generalized Anxiety Disorder

Again, it is important to distinguish the disturbance from so-called normal and transient concerns.

The distinctive character of this disorder is, in fact, the chronicity and pervasiveness of the anxious worry with its somatic correlates, and the lack of control of the worry, which does not allow the person to effectively manage the problems that, from time to time, nag his mind.

There is evidence of stressful life events in the onset of this type of disorder. The overlap and mutual influence with other anxiety and mood disorders is high, and the frequency in women is higher.

Panic Disorder

The panic attack manifests itself as a precise period of intense fear or discomfort, during which they develop suddenly, reaching a peak in about ten minutes, at least four of the following symptoms:

- palpitations, heart palpitations or tachycardia;
- sweating;
- fine tremors or large shocks;
- choking sensation;
- feeling of asphyxia;
- chest pain or discomfort;
- nausea or abdominal discomfort;
- sensation of skidding, instability, light-headedness or fainting;
- derealization (sense of unreality of the world) or depersonalization (feeling detached from oneself);
- fear of losing control or going mad;
- fear of dying;
- paraesthesia (feeling of numbness or tingling);
- chills or hot flashes.

Panic attacks are defined as caused by the situation, when they are strongly associated with triggering factors that are clearly identifiable, sensitive to the situation, when the association is less strong, and unexpected, when they appear in situations that do not justify them. To make a diagnosis of panic disorder, unexpected and recurrent attacks must be present, while the exclusive presence of attacks caused by the situation reflects the presence of a phobia.

Agoraphobia

Agoraphobia is defined as anxiety about being in places or situations from which it would be difficult or embarrassing to leave, or where help may not be available, in the case of a panic attack.

Agoraphobic fear refers to characteristic situations, which include:

- being away from home alone;
- being in a crowd or in a queue;
- being on a bridge.

Such situations are either actively avoided, or are endured with great discomfort and the expectation of a panic attack, or the presence of a chaperone is required.

22

CHAPER 3 • Symptoms of Anxiety

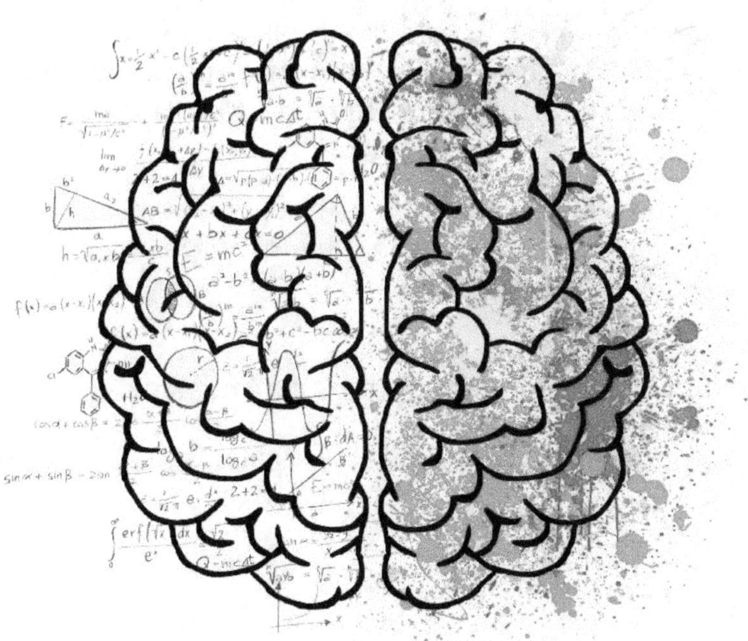

Cognitive Symptoms of Anxiety

From a cognitive point of view the typical symptoms of anxiety are:

- the sense of mental emptiness
- a growing sense of alarm and danger
- the induction of images, memories and negative thoughts
- the implementation of protective cognitive behaviors
- the marked sensation of being observed and of being at the center of others' attention.

Behavioral Symptoms of Anxiety

In the human species anxiety translates into an immediate tendency to explore the environment, in search of explanations, reassurances and escape routes. The main instinctive strategy of anxiety management is also the avoidance of the feared situation ("better safe than sorry" strategy).

Moreover, protective behaviors (being accompanied, taking anxiolytics when needed, etc.), and submissiveness are frequent.

Physical Symptoms of Anxiety

Anxiety is also often accompanied by physical and physiological manifestations such as:

- tension
- shaking
- sweat
- palpitation
- heart rate increase
- dizziness
- nausea
- tingling at the ends and around the mouth
- derealization and depersonalization.

Below we will better describe some physical symptoms of anxiety, how they occur and what are the possible consequences:

<u>Palpitations</u>

It is necessary, as far as possible, to distinguish different conditions related to palpitations: heart palpitations, tachycardia and arrhythmia.

The latter, for example, often occurs with irregular heartbeats even in healthy people during their daily activities and is more likely to occur when the person is anxious.

It can be induced by a number of agents such as nicotine, caffeine, alcohol and electrolyte imbalance.

Often the interpretation given to this physical symptom during an anxious state is related to the idea of having a heart attack. This even if at the base there is an increased electrophysiological excitability of the heart muscle that has no negative consequences from a medical point of view.

Chest pain

It is a physical symptom that can occur during periods of high anxiety in the absence of a heart condition.

It can therefore come from different sources such as chest breathing and gastrointestinal disturbances (ex. esophageal reflux or esophageal spasms). When the person interprets the benign causes of pain catastrophically, it is possible that the anxious state increases, leading to panic.

But in reality, we know that when a very high anxiety state emerges, the body secretes adrenaline which causes an increase in heartbeat and the body works faster. It is an evolutionary way to better prepare the person to handle dangerous situations.

If the adrenaline would damage the heart, how could man survive to this day? Therefore, the acceleration of the heartbeat due to anxious states does not cause heart attacks; there must be something pathological for this to happen.

Feeling of breathlessness

Breathing is an action that works regardless of what a person thinks or does, it is automatically controlled by the brain. In fact, brain controls also work when you try to stop breathing.

The feeling of shortness of breath is very frequent in anxiety disorders and results from prolonged and repeated chest breathing.

In fact, a physical response to stress is the relative dominance of chest breathing over abdominal breathing, which leads to fatigue of the intercostal muscles, which strain and have spasms that cause discomfort and pectoral pain inducing the feeling of shortness of breath.

If you cannot understand that these sensations are induced by chest breathing, then they will seem sudden, frightening, causing the person to become even more alarmed.

Nausea or abdominal disorders

The stomach contracts and relaxes regularly and constantly.

When this rhythm is disturbed, nausea occurs. Several factors can lead to this physical sensation such as ingestion of certain foods, vestibular disorders, postural hypotension or even previously neutral stimuli.

The function of diet and digestion are the first to block during an alert state, but if the person misinterprets nausea as a sign of impending vomiting, anxiety is more likely to increase and lead to panic.

But, fortunately, that nausea leads to vomiting rarely happens, people are more likely to overestimate this possibility.

Tremors and sweating

The first are involuntary, oscillating and rhythmic movements of one or more parts of the body, caused by the alternating contraction of opposite muscle movements.

Sweating instead helps to control body temperature, which rises when you have been anxious.

In fact, stress stimulates the sympathetic nervous system with increased levels of adrenaline and norepinephrine that stimulate an increase in metabolism, thus increasing heat production and the resulting sweating useful for lowering body temperature.

Again, the greater the attention to these physical symptoms the greater the likelihood that they will increase in intensity.

Dizziness

Dizziness is the product of the illusion of self-movement or the environment.

They consist of feelings of confusion or dizziness, dizziness or dizziness.

When information from the balance system (visual, somatosensory and vestibular system) comes into conflict, vertigo occurs.

Balance problems and associated physical symptoms (instability, anxiety, cold sweats, palpitations) can also occur as a result of anxiety, hyperventilation and common stress reactions such as tightening the jaw and teeth.

Obviously, the intensity of dizziness can increase if more attention is paid to these sensations.

Derealization or depersonalization

Depersonalization (feeling unreality) or depersonalization (feeling detached from oneself), are experiences that can be induced by fatigue, sleep deprivation, meditation, relaxation or the use of substances, alcohol and benzodiazepines.

There are also other more subtle causes related to short periods of sensory deprivation or reduction of sensory input, such as fixing a point on a wall for 3 minutes.

The curious thing is that, here too, the vicious circle is established according to the interpretation given to these physical symptoms. When you experience depersonalization or derealization (an experience that a third of the population has experienced) the more frightened a person is, the more they breathe, the more charged with oxygen (eliminating carbon dioxide) the more the feeling of depersonalization or derealization increases.

CHAPTER 4 • Anxiety Care

Psychotherapy

Psychotherapy It is important that people who live permanently in a state of fear and agitation know that, through psychotherapy, they can recover a sense of inner security and learn an ability to master reality, which can calm them and limit anxiety.

The psychotherapist, through an interview with the person, collects information aimed at understanding what aspects produce in the subject the experience of anxiety, as well as the degree of disability that the disorder creates in the individual.

Psychodynamic approach

From a therapeutic point of view, schematically there can be two ways to treat anxiety with psychotherapy: one is the cognitive-behavioural approach, which aims at treating the symptom in a short form. The other is the psychodynamic approach, used by me, for which anxiety never presents itself as a separate disorder, but always has to be associated with a personality organization within which this anxiety fits.

What does this mean exactly? We must consider anxiety as a positive signal, a bell that warns the person that there are some things to fix. When the burglar alarm rings in the house, we do not know if it rings because a mouse broke in, because the electrical system is broken or because a burglar broke in. Through psychotherapy, we have to understand what this alarm tells us, what in the person is not working well psychologically at this moment in history. What is happening? Usually there are some issues that the person has to face and is afraid, or does not have the tools, or that he has left out for a long time: anxiety becomes the bell that warns that the time has come to face them.

Pharmacological Treatment

The use of anxiolytic drugs is widespread: they are often considered "light" drugs while, like all psychoactive substances, they cause psychological and physical addictive effects, in addition to the need to increase the dose to feel their effects. In addition, prolonged use of tranquilizers can in the long term cause memory loss and may promote the onset of depression.

It should not be forgotten that anxiolytics do not treat the causes of anxiety: they make toothache go away, but they do not cure the infection. For this reason, they should only be used in emergency situations or for a limited period, for example in support of psychological therapy, perhaps at an early stage.

Never use them with self-prescribing: psychotropic drugs are real medicines, and should always be taken according to your doctor's prescription.

Food

While it is not possible to treat anxiety with food, certainly making some changes in your lifestyle, including nutrition, can help.

It is clear that there are some foods that can worsen states of tension: think of fried foods, high glycemic index carbohydrates, refined sugars, alcoholic beverages or nervous drinks.

Instead, there are foods that have an anti-stress function or that promote a state of relaxation.

At the base of an anti-stress diet there are fruits and vegetables, which help you to fight cellular oxidation and take all the vitamins and minerals necessary for your body to function properly.

Whole grains ensure an excellent intake of magnesium, which counteracts fatigue, anxiety and depression, zinc, which improves the ability to concentrate, and selenium, which stimulates your immune system.

All foods rich in Omega 3, such as blue fish, are also excellent. These "good fats" promote the vitality of the nervous system and have a positive effect on the cardiovascular system: you can also find them in almonds and walnuts.

Yes also in white meats, such as chicken and turkey: thanks to tryptophan, amino acid precursor of serotonin, they stimulate your good mood. Rich in tryptophan also milk, yogurt and cheese.

And then, of course, let's not forget the dark chocolate, which contains serotonin, useful to stabilize your mood and with excellent calming properties.

Natural Remedies

To combat apathy, restlessness, tiredness and difficulty concentrating, you can use some essential oils. good help against anxiety.

Or you can use plants and herbs that stimulate your tranquillity, such as chamomile, lemon balm and valerian, hawthorn and passion flower.

Don't forget that exercise is essential to stimulate the production of endorphins, the molecules of well-being that provide you with serenity. You can choose any sport, just have fun and let your mind go away from your thoughts.

In this sense very effective are the meditative disciplines, such as meditation, often based on breathing. They bring benefits related to a better management of anxiety, thanks to the lowering of cortisol levels, heart rate and blood pressure.

CHAPTER 5 • Insecurity in the Relationship

Falling in love and loving someone means taking a leap into the void and sharing the most intimate part of ourselves. This is why some people feel a strong insecurity in the relationship. To love means to have trust, let it flow and open up to another person.

The couple must be a safe place where they can express themselves and show who they really are without worry. If this is not possible, the relationship is likely to be poisoned by insecurity and doubt.

In this chapter we will focus on the signs of insecurity in the couple's relationship, which can occur when the relationship has already started or when it is considered over.

It should also be said that one of the signs of insecurity is to abandon "the playing field" a priori. So let's talk about when you know someone you like very much, but even before any kind of bond is formed, insecurity, dizziness, fear of being hurt or abandoned begin to emerge.

Running away when you are getting to know someone is a sign of insecurity known and identified by those who experience it first hand and those who suffer it. However, other signs of insecurity in the relationship can go unnoticed; we analyse them in the following paragraphs.

Insecurity starts from the inside and not from the outside

Although the justification of the insecure man and woman in love is always that it is the other person who creates insecurity, the truth is often that insecurity starts from within.

It is linked to a lack of self-esteem and self-confidence or the perception of low personal value.

And it is also linked to one's own sense of non-independence.

In other words: You are insecure when (and why) you depend too much on the other to be well, when having someone close to you is the main condition not to face the terror of not being loved by anyone, not even by yourself.

The inability to love each other is an ugly beast.

It leads us to find people who do not respect us, who feed our insecurities and give us serious reasons to be jealous.

It is therefore of little use to try to fix a relationship by trying to control the behaviour of the other.

What needs to be done instead is to learn to feel good about yourself first of all.

Signs of Insecurity in the Relationship

<u>Control and Jealousy</u>

One of the reactions caused by insecurity in the relationship is the search for control over the relationship (the things you do together) and the partner (what he does or stops doing). Some people have a very high need for control, i.e. they need a high degree of control in order not to feel threatened. We are talking about a need that often spills over to the partner.

Usually when one person tries to control another, they feel insecure. A very high need for control can apparently go hand in hand with psychological problems such as obsessive compulsive disorder.

Insecurity in a relationship also manifests itself in the form of jealousy. Sign of insecurity par excellence. Even people who are confident in their relationship and have confidence in themselves can be jealous, but without enough intensity or frequency to dominate them.

A good way to combat jealousy is to eliminate all behaviors that lead to this feeling. For example, ask your partner where he is, what time he will arrive, who he saw, look at his profile on social networks, etc.

Continue searching for signs of affection and love: "Tell me you love me".

Expecting continuous demonstrations of affection from the partner is a sign of insecurity in the relationship. It pleases everyone to receive affectionate demonstrations, but it is quite different to count the times that the partner makes an affectionate gesture.

Some people measure and compare the loving gestures they receive from their partner. They expressly ask the partner to express and quantify the love they feel.

People who feel insecure about their relationship use expressions such as "you are not as affectionate as you are with your friends" or "when we are at home, you do not show your affection and when we are in company you do. Signs of fear, insecurity and low self-esteem.

On the other hand, it must be considered that these evaluations are natural if made with little frequency. Those who are sure of themselves and their relationship understand that they go through different states and that each of them changes their disposition towards others, including the partner.

Dr. Megan McCarthy's research at the University of Waterloo states that when you have a low self-esteem the person tends not to talk about your needs so as not to annoy your partner. In most cases, however, this makes it difficult to create a healthy bond, as regrets, criticism and malaise may appear over time.

Do not express your opinions and avoid conflicts

Discussing and disagreeing with your partner is healthy. Disagreements and differences of opinion are necessary to learn to live with the other person. Each of us has our own characteristics and needs.

There are many people who try to dismiss any omen of discussion, thinking that this is a symptom of weakness within the couple. They thus avoid sharing their opinions to promote speeches that coincide with the ideas expressed by the partner.

This habit, which in the short term can be good for communication, ends up destroying the person and the couple in the long run. On the other hand, the lack of spontaneity, instead of eliminating insecurity in the couple's relationship, increases it.

The three signals we have just talked about are not only useful to identify insecurity in the couple relationship, they are also good strategies to change attitudes. The couple is an important pillar of well-being when they feel they can rely on it while remaining themselves. Otherwise, it generates great tension.

CHAPTER 6 • How to fight Insecurity in Love and Life

I know it can take a lifetime to learn to love each other and that is no small thing.

But when our insecurities make the other suffer there is nothing else to do but strive to do exactly the opposite of what would be natural to do, which is what we would do if we loved each other.

In other words:

- if insecurity leads you to be absent, make an effort to be present.
- When it leads you not to trust, try to trust.
- if it makes you be negative, strive to see the positive side of things.

Believe me, I know very well what it feels like not to be able to control the anxiety or bad habits that make you anxious or angry about stupid things.

But I also know that once you understand what aspects need to be improved, over time it becomes easier to control them.

Regardless of how they manifest themselves, insecurities in love can only be overcome by striving to be helpful, loving, understanding.

Take responsibility for your well-being

When you are sympathetic and leave room for your partner, paradoxically you make it more difficult for her to betray you or leave you.

If you are positive and affectionate with your partner you will make them appreciate you more, to feel lucky to have you.

By giving credit and importance to insecurities, instead, you are behaving in a diametrically opposite way.

When you get caught up in pride and negativity you stop doing your part in the relationship and you increase your expectations of the other.

In these cases you can even detach yourself thinking: "you made me feel bad so now you have to be the one to make me understand that you love me".

Only that no one has the power to put any emotion inside us.

If we feel bad it is because we have evil inside us.

It is a good rule of life, therefore, to focus on what we can do ourselves to make things better, not expect the other to do all the work.

The will of another human being is not something we can directly influence.

On the contrary, our reactions to the behavior of others are something over which we have full control.

Focus on your self-esteem first

The well-being that comes from your self-esteem is much more stable than the well-being that comes from having a partner.

Having self-esteem is a bit like having an independent gasoline reserve in addition to the common reserve.

Even if love ends or your partner chooses to leave you, the independent reserve will allow you to continue living through disappointment and pain of loss.

To fill the reserve with self-esteem and overcome insecurity the best thing to do is to work on your identity and get to know each other better.

Once you know who you are you can find passions and personal projects to undertake and, in doing so, enrich your life.

A fuller and richer life will allow you not only to have more things to share with your partner, but also to see your relationship as something to work on together rather than as your only source of oxygen.

Self-esteem and Personal Independence

A relationship in which both partners have a healthy level of personal security and independence will be a healthy relationship that will last.

A self-confident person will not try to control the other, will not behave in a jealous or irrational manner, will not blame the other for their own anxieties.

The self-confident person will have the stability and clarity of mind to focus on what the other person needs.

And when we pay attention to the other person, when we give her what she needs to feel loved, we solidify the relationship, revitalize it, save it.

This is the only way to overcome insecurities and strengthen the relationship.

All other strategies, shortcuts, are meant to pollute the relationship.

You can also ask your boyfriend to cancel himself from socials or you can forbid your girlfriend to go out, but if you really need these tricks to feel less insecure, it can mean that A. it's not true love or B. you need to work on yourself.

Focus on things you have control over, such as your sense of personal value, self-esteem and trust.

Remember that if you want to keep your partner close you will be much more effective if you learn to be more positive, loving, cheerful.

These are the qualities that attract, that represent a real panacea for a relationship.

Focus then on how much you are worth, on your strengths.

Ask yourself what you can give your partner that no one else can give him/her.

The answer you will give will be your lifeline from insecurities in love, it will help you to free yourself from their destructive influence.

Difference between Insecurity and Vulnerability

At the end of our speech, it is necessary to mention the very important difference between insecurity and vulnerability.

While the former, as we have said so far, can represent a trap for the relationship, the latter can instead help it.

Vulnerability is in fact a great way to build trust and intimacy in a relationship, as it presupposes an opening to the other person, a sharing of one's weaknesses without attacking or criticizing.

Then, thanks to the lack of criticism and tension, conversations become more open and the relationship deeper and more exclusive.

It is enriched by a better mutual knowledge and instills in the couple the desire to protect each other.

Unlike the insecure person, the person who has the courage to be vulnerable in a couple is projected towards the other, not towards themselves.

All this means only one thing: that everyone can be insecure and feel fragile, but what distinguishes us is the use we make of this fragility, especially in relationships.

On the one hand, there is the option to hide insecurities in love and try to control the partner to prevent him from leaving us (as we said before).

On the other hand, there is the choice to put our cards on the table, show our insecurities without accusing, without victimhood.

In the latter option, the shame that isolated us before turns into sharing, and leads us to fully live one of the fundamental aspects of life on this earth: feeling a connection with another human being.

Because in the end, without vulnerability there is no sense of belonging or closeness, and one cannot fully love or feel loved.

CHAPTER 7 • 10 Ways to Overcome Insecurity in the Relationship

I struggle to understand it, for what is my mentality, and thanks be to God, my strength, but I have realized over the years that too many people feel unworthy of love, for much of their lives.

A common question that hovers among them is:

"Why should anyone be interested in me?"

This relational insecurity shows problems that do not exist, turning what could have been a successful relationship into a short-lived, sad and traumatic failure.

Do you know the feeling?

If so, I want you to be as strong and serene as I am lucky enough to be.

<u>HERE'S HOW TO STOP FEELING INSECURE:</u>

1. **Stop thinking that everything is about you.**

An egocentric worldview will make you chase monsters where they don't exist. If your partner doesn't want to go out, don't assume that it's because of you, that he doesn't want to be with you, that he prefers everything else to you: he can just have a day that made him bullshit!

Take advantage of it: turn off the phone, fill the tub and pour a glass of wine.

Stop psychologically analyzing the words he has chosen to tell you that he doesn't want to go out, don't look for a message behind his tone, behind his gestures and his posture.

Obsessing with hidden meanings is an infallible way to miss the point and chase a monster that does not exist!

Don't blame your partner for being too quiet, or constantly ask him "what are you thinking about?", during every moment of silence.

The overwhelming need to fill every second of silence with (useless) words is a habit of the insecure person. And believe me: man is a simple mind. He is thinking of a bullshit (in a good, not derogatory sense), which has nothing to do with you!!!

Take your partner's hand, inhale, exhale and enjoy the moment of silence together.

Who says you can't feel good just being together, even in silence?

2. Stop obsessing

Your thoughts may be the best friends in your relationship or the absolute worst.

The quality of your thoughts has a direct effect on the quality of your relationship.

Have you ever gotten caught up in negative thoughts like "I know one day he'll get sick of me" or "How could they love me?".

These thoughts have little to do with reality, but they have a lot to do with fear.

In other words, the problem that concerns you does not exist: you invented it!

Whenever you feel insecure about your relationship, say to yourself: "The thing I am worried about only exists in my head. I am in full control of everything, and there is nothing I am afraid of, nothing!".

If you need an extra whiplash of strength, add to that: *"It is he who must fear losing me!*

3.   Stop dragging all that weight around with you...

Have you ever gotten out of a relationship so terrible that you would simply like to never think about it again? Do you think you are the only one and the most unfortunate? But stop it!

We would have an enormous difficulty in finding a person who doesn't drag a burden from a tragic relationship of the past, who is bigger, who is less.

Because you see, this love thing is an unpredictable and sometimes really bumpy road.

A small burden is okay, you also need to lighten the load before starting a new relationship. Forget any offensive feelings or residual resentment you may have left and realize that your new relationship is a new opportunity to put it all behind you.

4.   Stop seeing things in black and white

How do you react when someone accuses you for something you didn't do? Even without too many polls I would say that you move defensively, like everyone else.

In the same way, attacking your partner for a problem - no matter how obvious it may seem to you - will most likely make them get defensive.

This usually leads to a dragged-out "fight", which is the opposite of productive, because you are too busy trying to prove you are right instead of resolving the conflict (realistic or not...).

If you have a problem or a doubt or a simple melancholy, do not point the finger immediately, but rather approach your partner with understanding and desire for things to get better and better.

Rest assured that neither is fully right or wrong.

The real answer lies somewhere in the middle, between the two of you.

5.   Stop being paranoid

Let's face it: we all talk to people of the opposite sex. It would be better if it wasn't so!

Just because a boy and a girl are friends or acquaintances, it doesn't mean there is anything else in their relationship.

Avoid the temptation to spy on their phone, Facebook messages or email account.

While this may temporarily calm your nerves when you don't see that there is actually nothing to see, it is also behavior that could quickly become engaging, habitual, and therefore highly damaging to the relationship when you find out.

6.   Stop putting off uncomfortable conversations.

While conflicts are stressful in the moment, they also build the strength of your long-term relationship.

Dealing with your (your) problems without fear, but with maturity and willingness, will help you get closer and closer.

Don't say words for others, but speak with sincerity and clarity, and so should he.

You will develop a confidence so strong that you can tell your partner everything that is on your mind... until you read it to yourself!

7.   Do not look for certainties a priori

There is no manual that explains how relationships should be. Each story is unique and unrepeatable. But undoubtedly, the temptation to want the certainty that things will go well because you are following the "manual of love" well, is tempting to the insecure. In fact, when things are not as we think they should be, we lose control because we do not have the tools to understand and decipher reality. In these cases the watchword is: relax! Stop controlling everything and leave yourself the opportunity to get to know the other person and get to know yourself in a new relationship.

8.   Let your partner have his or her space

To be happy as a couple it is essential that both partners commit themselves, each as they can and as they are. You do not have the right to expect everything to be the way you want it to be or to expect your partner to live the relationship according to rules you have imposed without discussion, just to feel safe. Mutual trust and respect are earned little by little and so is love. The fact that you have found someone you are comfortable with does not mean that everything has been said and the cards are already all on the table. The relationship needs to grow. Let the other person also have a chance to express himself. If you are too suffocating, the relationship will never really blossom.

9.   Stop assuming what the other person is thinking.

This problem affects many interpersonal relationships, not only love ones. We often believe we know what the other person is thinking and we act accordingly. This, without asking what the problem is or assuming that we have understood before the other may have opened his mouth to tell us his thought. Once again, this is fantasy and confuses reality.

10. Stop depending on anyone but yourself.

Essential point!

Having someone to hug, kiss, cuddle, make love and share life with, make plans, imagine the future is nothing short of wonderful.

But before heading off into the sunset in search of love, you must learn to love yourself!!!

Just like you shouldn't invite a friend to your house when it seems there has just been a police raid, no matter how messy it is, you shouldn't let anyone into your life while it is still upside down.

Take care of yourself, the house of your heart, before inviting someone else into it.

If you let go of the insecurity, you can expect some wonderful side effects: an enormous serenity and a textbook love story!

CHAPTER 8 ● Negative Thoughts: How to Eliminate Them?

What I explain will be very practical and you can start training your mind right away.

Consider this: you don't have to change your thoughts, but change the way you think for the better, how you use your mind.

Another mistake is convincing you to "think too much". Actually we never think too much, but we do it wrong. And soon you will know how to stop doing it forever.

How negative thoughts are born

The first thing you need to understand is the link between thought and emotion. And that explains why negative thoughts are so annoying.

Each of your emotions, without exception, depends on what you think. This is called emotional independence.

Basically it works like this: whatever you may experience (situations, words, events, behavior of others and everything else), is judged by your mind.

There are only two possibilities: positive judgment when what you see seems good for you, and negative judgment if it seems bad for you.

A negative thought is but a negative judgment about something. And therefore it always generates negative emotions.

The reason why negative thoughts are so limiting is precisely this: they are the source of all our malaise.

But are these thoughts yours? Are they yours?

Many people write to me because they have negative and "ugly" thoughts, they think unpleasant things even towards important people they love.

There are two important things to understand: you are not your thoughts.

Here I am interested in reassuring you: you are the person who creates a thought, who controls it. The thoughts are yours in the sense that you have the full power (at least potential!) to do whatever you want with them.

But you are not your thoughts and you can change them, transform them, throw them out of your mind or cultivate them by making them strong and important.

You hold the helm of your life through your thoughts. The negative ones don't have to scare you, you need instead to understand them (never be afraid of your own thoughts!) and learn to choose.

In fact it is you who decide what to keep in your mind and what to throw away, a bit like when some things you don't need to throw in the trash.

The problem with negative thoughts, in fact, is that although they are under your control, you usually find them in your mind without consciously choosing them.

Soon I will also explain how our unconscious works.

First, however, consider that these negative thoughts are born because of the stimuli that bombard our mind: television, places, people, speeches, words, situations, images and much more.

Your mind is like a big antenna that picks up signals coming from outside. Everything around us becomes a stimulus that leads us to think in a certain way.

And we often think in a negative way.

We see a situation and evaluate it as positive or negative, in the same way we evaluate the things that others say, the words heard in a film, the scenes we see on television and so on.

But there is more: our mind is also like a camera that is "impressed" by everything it comes into contact with.

That is to say that what we see, feel, perceive through our senses, leaves a mark (impresses in this sense) in our mind.

And the stronger and more repeated is a certain stimulus, the greater is the sign it leaves.

So it is normal that if we continuously see violent images on television, they will become familiar to us, and our thoughts will be easily influenced by this type of stimulus.

Our mind is also like a sponge and easily absorbs everything it comes into contact with.

If we spend a lot of time with a person who uses a particular language, whether it is vulgar, for example, or much sought after in reverse, we will begin to absorb this way of speaking.

Our mind captures everything around us and every little detail becomes a stimulus that leads us to think in a certain way.

And the truth is that we are bombarded by mostly negative images: deaths, accidents, violence, corruption, degradation, infidelity, superficiality, wealth as an end in itself.

Our culture passes to each of us clear and usually negative messages:

- ✓ If you want to succeed, you have to be good-looking.
- ✓ Aesthetically beautiful people are always stupid and unprepared.
- ✓ You don't make a career without recommendations or compromises.
- ✓ Everyone is selfish and ready to cheat you: you cheat them first!
- ✓ You can't trust anyone.

- ✓ You can't trust your own ideas: if others are against it, you are wrong.
- ✓ Who are you to deserve to be happy?
- ✓ You are worth it if you have money, power and economic and business success.
- ✓ If you are a woman, everyone will treat you like a sexual object.
- ✓ You must do what others expect otherwise they will misjudge you.
- ✓ If you want love, you must conform to others and not be yourself, or yourself.
- ✓ We are not free to choose, but we must adapt ourselves to life.
- ✓ Life is a struggle, exhausting and full of bills and costs.
- ✓ To some everything, to others nothing (and you are among others!).

These are some of the basic rules that our society wants us to share. And usually we succeed well.

In fact before I explained that every thought generates an emotion and that negative ones are the cause of negative emotions. Well, but there is more.

Behind every negative thought of yours there is a rule. One like the ones I just listed.

Basically you observe what happens to you and think in a negative way every time your rules tell you that it is right to do this. Then you generate negative emotions and malaise.

All negative emotions come from fear

Fear is at the basis of every negative emotion, and it is the one we feel most often, without perhaps recognizing it.

As you see behind every negative thought there is a world of rules and patterns and every negative (or positive) thought of yours depends basically on how you observe your life, on the rules you think are right.

While convincing us that all these negative thoughts are always and only children of childhood trauma, you have to start to understand that every thought comes from how you live your life.

There is not a single thought that is in your past. What's more, the past counts for absolutely nothing.

What determines your thoughts is what today is your way of living life, the rules you believe to be true, the reality you think you have to deal with.

The real problem with negative thoughts is to move from thinking, which being negative causes you discomfort, to its meaning: what does it tell you? Why do you think this? Does it correspond to reality?

There are two types of negative thinking, let's say so: thoughts that reflect reality, that is, those that are negative but are based on concrete facts.

And then those that instead arise from impressions, feelings, preconceptions, personal patterns and that dictate a vision of things that does not correspond to the reality we really live.

As you read in the example taken from my book, each of us tends to see reality according to our own rules, instead of questioning them by observing the facts.

In a little while I will also explain how to keep any negative thoughts at bay, avoiding them to paralyze you, but only if you learn to understand reality and act constructively, you can really eliminate them.

If you are faced with a real problem, you have to solve it and negative thinking will no longer make sense.

If instead you observe and misjudge reality because of your prejudices, you have to get in touch with what is really happening and change your view of things.

I will also teach you how to develop a different, positive way of thinking, in the sense that it allows you to deal with every situation, no matter how difficult, uncomfortable or painful, without feeling bad anymore.

In fact, always remember this: I want to be happy. And you want to be happy too.

When I explain what happiness is, I emphasize that it is about well-being, serenity, calm, positive emotions. Something we all desire.

You can try it even in the midst of problems and difficulties, as long as you free yourself from negative thoughts and have a positive and balanced way of thinking.

Now I will explain how the unconscious decides your thoughts, then how not to let the negative ones overwhelm you, finally how to eliminate them forever from your way of life.

How your mind decides the things you think

To totally eliminate negative thoughts you must understand that each of them is basically a habit.

If every morning, at 9 a.m., I have breakfast with a friend of mine, my mind will begin to associate at 9 a.m. this event.

If after so many months we don't have breakfast anymore, every time it will be 9 a.m. I will still think about breakfast, my friend and everything that was there in this shared moment.

The mind has learned to associate to a time, to the bar where we had breakfast, to the croissant that she always took, certain thoughts and certain memories.

And we do this all the time: words and names with which others call us, places, sounds, perfumes, music, objects, places.

All this becomes a stimulus to thoughts because over time the mind has learned to associate them with something.

A thought thus becomes a habit.

If I listen to some offspring my mind automatically starts a certain song that is strongly associated with those words. And I think it happens to you too.

Once you get in touch with it, it is as if you start the record. Like the old Jukeboxes where you press a button and the chosen song starts.

Or like the soda and snack or coffee machines, where you type the right lyrics and the machine returns the soda or snack you want.

That's also how it works in the back of your mind: launch the right "song" when something asks for it. And it's often words, places, people, or other stimuli that you have associated with something.

Every habit is created by repeating something so many times that our mind proceeds automatically, on an unconscious level, because it already knows where to go in front of a certain stimulus.

We are constantly bombarded by millions of stimuli, because everything around us is a stimulus.

Our mind can only handle a small part of all this information, at least on a conscious level. Most of it, in fact, is perceived without us being aware of it.

Our unconscious manages almost all the stimuli we receive from the world and allows us to pay attention only to the (few) important things, working for us on everything else.

The more you repeat certain thoughts, the stronger they will be and our mind will automatically repeat them in front of certain stimuli.

When a relationship ends, for example, there will be a lot of things that suggest thoughts and memories of that person. We may really be surrounded by stimuli that make us suffer.

But it is not the things you see the problem: but the habit of your mind to recall certain thoughts in front of objects, words, places, sounds.

All this is fundamental if you want to forget a love that is over or if you want to understand how we fall in love, for example.

Everything you experience in your life is related to a thought and our thoughts are often unconscious, based on habits and patterns that you have cultivated over time.

Even if you don't realize it, these thoughts remain stored and are recalled whenever your unconscious deems it useful, because it has learned that it is right.

Also, in the case of negative thoughts, you must consider that they respond to possible dangerous situations, so they are indispensable to deal with life's risky situations.

As said, a negative thought does not always correspond to something really dangerous, but the unconscious does not make assessments, it does not know how to distinguish a danger.

Our unconscious is basically an automatic pilot that reproposes what it has learned to be better for us.

Remember that a negative thought is such because you have a negative judgment of something. But there are very few things that are objectively negative.

In most cases (almost always!), we think negatively about situations that are not negative, but that we live as such.

And I repeat: our unconscious does not decide this, but simply follows our rules and acts on the basis of what we consider positive or negative.

You have decided, over time and without paying attention to it, in what way today your unconscious automatically "starts" every thought.

With all the bombardment of negative stimuli we receive every day, it is obvious that our mind can offer us negative thoughts and a negative vision of situations and problems.

The secret is not to think that you are your thoughts. You create every thought and it is up to you to decide what to think and what to keep out of your mind.

As you saw in the previous video, every thought is born on the basis of rules and a precise vision of life: the unconscious follows this pattern, that's all.

To eliminate negative thoughts you have to change the rules and vision of things, you have to come to a different approach to reality, as said.

But before explaining how to do it, I'll explain how to manage negative thoughts immediately and stop them as soon as they occur.

How to stop them in less than 5 minutes

What you need to do is build a "safety net", which is a series of simple exercises to put into practice that will allow you to immediately dismiss negative thoughts.

And consequently also the negative emotions that sometimes block you.

The goal is to divert your mind from the negative thoughts that are the cause of the negative emotions and malaise we experience, and the secret is to find simple, independent but effective ways.

You can invent anything, as long as it really has the ability to keep your mind occupied, really distract you from negative thoughts, do not become a "little addiction" over time.

Here are my favorite exercises:

1. Look for the positive things around you: look at what's around you and make a list (written or aloud) with all the positive things you see and why you noticed them compared to everything else.

2. Look for the colored things around you: for example, everything that has the color red. You can write it down or just name each object out loud. And any color is fine.

3. Count and do calculations in your mind: for example, calculate the result of $15 + 36$. Then add 45, and then 125 and so on. Imagine the numbers in the column, add them up, and of course you can subtract or even brush up the tables (maybe backwards!).

4. Speak loudly, as if you were on the phone with someone and tell them what you are doing or a positive episode that happened to you or something you are passionate about.

5. Sing out loud the songs you prefer, but that are cheerful and put you in a good mood. With the same logic you can also pray out loud, as long as it is a dialogue with God and not prayers that you recite from memory.

6. Count the leaves attached to a branch, the grapes, the stones in the street, the number of cars you meet, or the mopeds, bakeries or anything else you can see around you.

7. Watching a funny video on YouTube: laughing helps your mind so much to leave negative thoughts behind.

Why does it work?

Because each of these exercises forces your mind to focus on something specific and distract it, as a result, from negative thoughts that weigh you down and make you feel bad.

For this network to work really well, however, follow some advice:

- ✓ Prefer things you can always do, in your mind, wherever you are and without the help of anyone.
- ✓ Try and find the exercise that works for you, that really takes your mind off other thoughts.
- ✓ If something you see that doesn't work, and your mind gets stuck on negative thoughts, change the exercise!
- ✓ Identify the most critical moments, the ones when negative thoughts attack you most often and prepare one of the exercises knowing that you will use it at that very moment, in that place or when you meet certain people.

Build your "safety net" now, and start using it often. This will help you to weaken the habit of negative thoughts.

Beware that this is not a permanent solution, but an "emergency response" against moments when you feel sick and need to react, a way not to be blocked by negative thoughts and emotions.

In fact, I explained to you that our mind gets used, in front of certain stimuli, to create negative thoughts because of how we see things and judge them.

Interrupting a habit is essential to be able to eliminate it, but it is not enough.

It takes a new awareness; you have to open your eyes and observe reality in a new way. I assure you that you can eliminate negative thoughts if you do this.

This does not take away that sometimes they will come back, but if your way of thinking changes and your mind becomes strong, they will be insignificant.

How to eliminate negative thinking

We will always feel negative emotions (due to negative thinking!) if we live something like an injustice.

If you want to eliminate negative thinking in a total and definitive way, it is not enough to distract yourself for a few minutes every time they occur: you have to turn them into positive thoughts.

I believe that 99.9% of the events you will experience will not be negative per se. They will only be negative if you live them as something wrong, ugly and unfair.

In fourth grade I was shy, but I told my parents what was going on, I was able to stay calm while a kid could choke me, I did not bear a grudge even then.

Why should I consider the negative things and not the positive things of that same episode?

Negative thoughts are not born because of an "ugly and bad" reality, but according to how you see it, how you look at it, the meaning you give it.

A martyr was someone who would rather die than deny his idea, his faith. For him it was more positive to die than to deny.

Death is not something negative either: it is a natural fact.

We all die, someone dies around us every day, nature is a continuous cycle of life and death.

A few days ago, joking, I was saying that the worms seen on the corpse of a mouse found in the countryside, are the same ones that will eat me, or you, at our time.

It is true, death is not something negative, but something natural, an integral part of life. We should not be afraid to die.

Negative thoughts are not related to the things you live, but to how you do it and if you want to eliminate them you have to change your vision of reality, your point of view.

You eliminate negative thoughts not by changing reality or distracting yourself, but by deeply transforming the way you think, becoming aware and learning to see things from different angles that you probably don't notice today.

My book, Emotional Independence, accompanies you in this process.

The problem is not what happens or what happened in the past, but how you live and remember everything, the meaning you give to each event.

If I understand the strength and calm with which I faced the "bully", if the guy on a sailing boat understand the determination and strength with which he handled a difficult situation well, then the negative thought dissolves.

There is no manipulation or self-suggestion, but a new, more real and deeper way of seeing things and understanding reality.

Obviously if negative thoughts are related to situations to be faced, you have to learn how to solve problems. And develop self-esteem and confidence in your abilities.

Leads you to positive thinking

You can start changing your perception of things right away by stopping placing distorted filters between you and the things you experience.

Key number 1: Negative to challenging.

Instead of considering something "positive", start calling it simple, comfortable or easy. And what you would call "negative" today must become uncomfortable, complicated, challenging.

Why is it important?

Because when you think something is "negative" you are not looking at objective reality, but you are applying a filter that is in your head.

Does being born without arms seem negative to you?

There are people who are born like that and learn to use their feet to do everything that people normally do using their arms and hands.

Negative? Maybe, but it's certainly more complicated for you. For people born without a hand is "normal", you have always been like that and you are used to using only one.

But when you put the label "negative" you no longer see an objective situation that makes something more complicated, you see malaise, something unfair, and you feel bad.

And defining something negative changes it? Does suffering for an objective condition change it?

No, you are just sick and you keep the problem to face. Eliminate the adjective "negative", replace it with complicated, demanding, difficult.

Stop loading yourself with negativity in the events you live and think about living them, how to deal with them in a constructive way.

Reality is not negative. It's reality, it's us who color it or live it in black and white.

Key number 2: from unfair to "we will see".

A friend of mine suffered a theft in the store and this, thanks to the payment of the insurance, turned out to be a fortune because that money allowed him to save his house.

10 years ago I was "unfairly" fired. But if I had not suffered this event today, I would not be here writing and you could not read me.

A journalist kicked a Syrian refugee who was carrying his son. Episode that bounced the man's story internationally, and earned him an employment contract in Spain.

If you want, I can give you more examples of how what we judge to be "unfair" today may turn out to be positive tomorrow.

Neither you nor I are able to judge whether something is right or wrong. I don't know what will happen in 10 minutes, can I know if what I see now is unfair?

What if it turns out to be the best thing in the world?

From today don't think that something is "unfair", think instead: "we will see".

And watch what could happen, doing your best to turn every situation into an opportunity.

Key number 3: from why to how

Why should a young boy attack a younger child by threatening him?

I don't know, but that child has the opportunity to pull out strength and courage from that episode.

Why does a man have to find himself in the middle of a storm on his way home in a sailboat, perhaps without having who knows what experience?

I don't know, but that man has the opportunity to put himself to the test, learn more about his limits, grow, gain experience, help those in trouble.

Why does the earthquake have to tear down my house?

I don't know, but I have the opportunity to help those who are living the same experience, give a hand to help those in need, rebuild my house and discover that nothing can stop me if I don't stop.

From today don't ask yourself why it was your turn, ask yourself how you can use that episode to do something positive.

Turn every situation, difficult or simple, into an opportunity. See what can happen and ask yourself:

- ✓ How can I make a contribution?
- ✓ How can I use this situation to my advantage?
- ✓ How can I make a difference?

As you can see, I'm showing you small steps to change your perspective.

The world is not the problem. It is how you look at it, how you live it.

If the problem is real, you just have to face it and stop loading your life with negative thoughts (and therefore emotions). It is not necessary and nothing changes.

Nothing has to change for you to be happy. Only you, only your mind.

Negative thoughts are not a problem, they are a way of thinking, living, understanding reality, the result of your vision of life, of the rules you believe to be true.

CHAPTER 9 • The Attachment Style

The primary mother-child relationship represents the prototype of future love relationships. The relationship with the parental figures of childhood conditions and determines our attachment model, i.e. the way we prepare ourselves on a cognitive, emotional and behavioral level to live all future relationships, including those of couples.

Attachment - described by Bowlby- is a biological, innate and evolutionary predisposition to search for the closeness of the parent and is expressed through the search for contact and the maintenance of physical closeness to the figure of attachment, anxiety and protest when it moves away. There are four different models of attachment to the parent that influence our sentimental relationships:

- secure attachment
- ambivalent insecure
- insecure avoiding
- disorganized attachment.

Safe Attachment

Safe attachment is characterized by a feeling of trust and security towards the parent. The child learns that the mother will satisfy his needs for nutrition, protection, physical contact, reassurance in states of tension. He has internalized the internal object: he knows that if the mother disappears from his field of vision, she will come back to care for him and will not abandon him.

Thanks to this confidence in the responsiveness of the parent, the individual feels serene in exploring the environment: he can play in peace with his peers, experience new situations without being assailed by anxiety and venture free from fears and conditioning in the journey of life.

The mother who is able to establish a model of secure attachment, is the "good enough" mother described by Winnicott: that is, she is a subject who has developed awareness of herself and her emotions in playing the maternal role. She is loving and caring towards her child, but at the same time she is not intrusive and intrusive: when the child does not manifest needs, she leaves him free to build an autonomous identity separate from her, without constantly and inappropriately intervening, suffocating and invading him.

Safe attachment and sentimental relationships

In romantic relationships the child who has developed a secure attachment will be able to give and receive love because he has internalized both roles: just as the mother has given everything for him, now he in the couple, identified in the maternal functions, is ready to give, care and protect the partner, but at the same time he knows how to receive care and love from them, without compromising his sense of independence and autonomy.

Moreover, as when he was a child, he trusted that his mother would return to him, she would not abandon him, in the romantic relationship he trusts that the partner will not abound and be faithful to him. People who are confident have a positive view of themselves and others, are optimistic and confident and easily abandon themselves to intimacy and dependence on others. They are welcoming, sincere and selfless. Trust and the ability to give oneself are the basis of the possibility of falling in love and making people fall in love (Hazan, Shaver, 1995).

Safe people generally prefer an emotional relationship with those who are equally safe and therefore able to respond adequately to their emotional needs. They have a remarkable ability to negotiate positions and conflicts; they describe their love stories as happy, friendly and based on mutual trust; they express their ability to accept and support their partner, despite their faults, and they have more lasting and stable relationships.

Insecure - ambivalent attachment

The insecure - ambivalent attachment is instead characterized by an underlying ambivalence in the relationship with the parent, a feeling of love and hate. If the mother has problems of her own, unresolved, she will live this very first relationship with her son in an ambivalent way: she unconsciously fears to be worn out by this little being so pretentious and demanding that she can manifest her needs in a clear and nonchalant way.

So on the one hand she will spoil her child to the point of suffocating him, but then, when the feeling of being consumed by him arises, she will frustrate him abruptly and excessively. If the mother spoils the child excessively and suffocates him, he does not learn to know how to wait and does not acquire the confidence that after the state of tension, pain and need will follow the satisfaction and relaxation of tension. The child learns a feeling of distrust, distrust and unreliability towards the parent, sometimes he is loving and helpful, sometimes he is inexplicably frustrating, bad, absent, detached, oppressive, suffocating. He himself when the parent is loving and caring will feel good, when the parent is rejecting or intrusive will feel bad.

Insecure attachment - ambivalent and sentimental relationships

These feelings of distrust, ambivalence towards oneself and the other, will extend into the relationship with the partner. In fact, he too will be perceived as loving at times, at others as detestable, he will be constantly suspected of him, he will always be feared that the other may unexpectedly interrupt the relationship or that he may betray. For a lack of self-esteem and a negative perception of oneself, one does not feel worthy of love and care and one doubts one's own value.

People with insecure-ambivalent attachment are individuals who often do not feel understood, are constantly afraid of being left by their partner or not being loved, have little confidence in themselves and in the other. In emotional relationships they are dependent and are unable to express their needs explicitly because the core of their relational dynamics is the fear of loss or rejection.

In living a couple relationship they highlight great difficulties because of their unconscious conflict between the symbiotic need to merge with the partner and the anguish that the realization of this fusion entails. Hence their explosions of anger, jealousy and suspicions about the partner's alleged unreliability and emotional distance. Their efforts to create meaningful relationships are governed, emotionally, by a sense of loss and insecurity.

They fall in love easily, but find it difficult to meet true love, experienced as something alternating and discontinuous. They live love as an obsession, characterized by emotional ups and downs, intense sexual attraction and strong feelings of jealousy towards their partner.

Avoiding attachment

In avoiding attachment, the mother is not very responsive to the needs of physical contact manifested by the child: she does not embrace him, does not pamper him, does not reassure him physically in moments of tension.

She has a cold and detached attitude, she is only concerned with satisfying the child's physical needs for nutrition and hygiene, neglecting emotional needs. It encourages the child to an early autonomy and independence, giving an exaggerated importance to self-sufficiency.

The child learns to calm himself or herself because he or she has understood that he or she cannot expect comfort from the parent. To implement this process of self-reassurance, the child blocks and freezes his emotions and distances himself more and more from the emotional world: what matters is rationality, emotions are potentially dangerous, expecting something from the other makes them fragile and vulnerable and it is preferable to get by on their own.

Avoiding attachment and sentimental relationships

When this attachment pattern extends into sentimental relationships, you will prefer to establish superficial relationships in which you do not let yourself get too involved. You will want to put an impassable wall between yourself and the other, preserving your own spaces of freedom and autonomy.

It is frequent the choice to live relationships in which everyone lives separately, considering cohabitation and marriage as a bond of closeness and intimacy excessive, which you are unable to support because it conflicts with your need for emotional independence.

People with insecure - avoiding attachment are characterized by fear of intimacy, emotional ups and downs, feelings of jealousy towards their partner. They tend to choose people similar to them as companions: their relationship has a good chance of holding on for a long time, considering the mutual need to distance themselves and the need to get involved as little as possible.

They are individuals who have a positive self-evaluation but a negative consideration of the other: the need to protect themselves from disappointment leads to avoid too ardent and passionate relationships and to preserve a feeling of independence and unassailability, emphasizing autonomy and self-confidence. Avoiding people often claim they have never been in love and consider their love stories as not very intense.

Disorganized attachment

Finally, the last attachment pattern is the one defined as "disorganized". It is the relational prototype more pathological and dangerous for the psychic balance of the subject, frequently connote the attachment of borderline subjects or with personality disorders.

The parent is often abusing, devaluing, totally incoherent and in default with respect to the parental role. It arouses in the child responses of fear and anguish. However, the child cannot do without the parent and binds affectively, despite the abuse and threats suffered.

The child develops attachment and desires emotional closeness from the very person who frightens and distresses him/her. The confusion that derives from the feelings of love and fear addressed to the figure of attachment, make the subject totally incapable of internalizing a tranquilizing and reassuring internal image of himself and the other. Both the self and the other are perceived as evil.

Disorganized attachment and sentimental relationships

When this pattern of attachment extends to the life of the couple, it results in highly dysfunctional relationships of the victim-executioner, sadistic-masochist type.

Disorganized individuals are victims of their own contradiction and discontinuity and hardly ever manage to be accepted as sentimental partners, if not by those who possess similar peculiarities. They feel a deep conflict between the need to maintain intimate, morbid ties, fusional involvement with the partner and the simultaneous need to keep him at a distance to avoid the threat of abandonment with the consequent emotional suffering. The sentimental relationship is experienced in a conflictual way, causing a strong anguish that one is unable to sustain.

Anxious attachment or elusive partner?

There are relationships in which anxiety is the predominant element, because one or both partners feel a sort of deep distrust towards the other. Sometimes this is due to the so-called anxiety attachment that some people develop towards the partner; others because the partner is elusive or indolent.

The anxious attachment outlines a bond in which restlessness, possessiveness and insecurity predominate. Typically, such a relationship is established because of unresolved problems of one or both partners. Other times, however, an anxious behavior is triggered or fueled by one of the two members.

Although there is basic insecurity, the person who feels it is not always the one who fuels or activates this type of relationship. In other words, sometimes the couple's relationship becomes a cause of anxiety because of the partner's attitude.

It is not easy to distinguish a case of an anxious attachment from one where the anxiety is triggered by a partner is elusive. For this reason, many people are unable to answer the question: "Is it my insecurity that leads me to feel anxiety towards my partner or is it my partner who is behaving in a way that would make anyone anxious?

Anxious attachment in the couple

Anxious attachment, also called insecure-ambivalent attachment, defines a bond in which there is a great desire for intimacy with the partner, but at the same time there is a deep fear of losing him. This feeling leads to an apprehensive experience of any manifestation, however minimal, of estrangement or rejection.

The anxious person, in fact, interprets so many behaviors that they do not actually indicate estrangement or rejection. By living each situation in this way, a great distrust of the partner and everything about him prevails. Often there is a disproportionate reaction to behavior that is completely normal.

In these cases, the partner's reaction is decisive. Ideally, one should adopt a sympathetic attitude and understand that the partner's or partner's anxiety stems from deep insecurity and sometimes unresolved psychological trauma.

A person suffering from an anxious attachment needs warmth, understanding and security. If you learn to trust your partner, your anxiety will most likely decrease.

The elusive partner

Those who have an anxious attachment do not need a person to take charge of their insecurities and fears, let alone relate to those who raise them. An elusive partner, in fact, feeds the anxiety of the person with whom he is with and strengthens the attachment, which is only harmful.

Many times he does so without realizing it, but he can also turn the relationship into a power play against the partner. An elusive partner is someone who, faced with conflict, flees or remains silent.

And so is someone who tries to solve problems hurriedly without deepening what is happening or who intellectualizes everything by preventing emotions from surfacing. It is also who irritates or feels uncomfortable when the partner cries or suffers.

Another characteristic of the elusive personality is the lack of emotion. For those who are anxious, it is harmful to have as a partner a person who has difficulty in having a relationship, who hates commitments or who does not want to have ties.

There are also those who ridicule or minimize their partner's emotions; this attitude increases their insecurities.

Whose fault is it?

Many times it is difficult to tell if the couple is made up of a member who suffers from chronic anxiety attachment, with all the consequences of the case, or if there is a normal attachment that becomes anxious because the partner says and does things that increase the unresolved insecurities of the partner.

To answer the question of whether an anxious attachment or avoidant behavior prevails in a relationship, it is important to identify the fears that are certain:

- Fear that the partner does not want to engage.
- Fear that a conflict cannot be resolved because the other person refuses to face it.
- Fear of not being heard or understood by the partner.
- Fear of being vulnerable.

If one of these fears is present, the partner is probably elusive. Other fears, especially if they are intense, indicate the predominance of an anxious attachment rather than an elusive partner. We refer to the fear of losing the other person, that our partner may fall in love with someone else, that he or she may stop loving us, or the fear of being alone.

Symptoms and Causes of Affective Dependence

To heal emotional dependence the first step is to recognize the symptoms and overcome them.

Let's start with the main symptoms:

- addiction: it seems obvious, but the first symptom of emotional addiction is the addiction itself. The affective-dependent pours over the other all its mechanisms of self-regulation, such as maintaining self-esteem, personal cohesion or feeling emotion. If the partner moves away from these personal properties are missing and the person who suffers from addiction can suffer exaggeratedly and panic.

- Inability to handle a possible separation. As mentioned above, the partner becomes vital to the emotional employee and separation is unimaginable pain.

- The dependent emotional person is easily blackmailed, precisely because he or she cannot conceive of separation, he or she would accept anything not to finish a story. At this point obviously the greatest danger is to lose their identity.

- Search for narcissistic people, because they represent exactly their opposite and are attracted by the false security and perfection that seem to emanate.

- The employee is subjugated and obliging to the partner, to the point that he or she can come to comply, worship and adore him or her, hoping to receive an acknowledgement that will probably never come.

The **causes of addiction** (as mentioned above) have deep roots and date back to childhood, when the child begins to build his or her own identity, and if there is criticism, punishment or complete indifference from the parents during this process, the child may grow up with a marked sense of guilt and low self-esteem.

Among the many family cases that can lead to the creation of low self-esteem, we can highlight two in particular:

- overprotective parents who have never believed in their children. Overprotective parents tend to satisfy all the needs and requirements of their children, without them having to think about anything. In this way children will grow up with little autonomy and independence, and probably even as adults, they will look for people who solve things for them on the one hand and on the other hand they will pour a lot of expectations on the partner giving him the power to be the only one who can solve his problems.

- Absent parents: Parents did not give the child those answers and confirmations to his emotional needs that he needed, leading him to feel incapable and worthless. In this case the partner represents that possibility of redemption and being loved. The loss of the partner could lead to a sense of loneliness and deep despair that could also lead to depression.

- These situations will lead the emotional employee to a loss of himself, in favor of the relationship, but being toxic, it can only lead to an even more pronounced loneliness and without identity. Precisely because self-esteem and identity are built by growing, emotional dependence can be considered a consequence of a failure in building self-esteem. If some symptoms of emotional dependence seem familiar to you, let's try to deepen the way to heal from emotional dependence.

How to recover from emotional addiction?

If you have found yourself caught up in a relationship that seems to be leading to an emotional addiction and you do not know how to get out of it, we leave you 4 tips to start getting rid of that addiction.

In order to slowly move away from this disorder, it is necessary that it is the same person who suffers from it to take steps towards the solution to overcome the emotional dependence.

Here are four tips to recognize it and get rid of it:

- Accept that you have a problem: There is no cure if the person who suffers from emotional dependence does not admit that they have a problem with their relationship. It is necessary to remember that this type of disorder is not only related to relationships but also to other types of people such as friends or family. If you recognize yourself in the description of the symptoms, it is time to find a solution.

- Make a list: After recognizing the disorder, you need to become aware of its consequences. It may be helpful to make a list of all the things you have done for the other person and that have caused you harm. In this way, you can understand that this form of addiction leads to actions that do not increase our well-being but worsen our lives with the sole objective of not losing the other. To combat emotional dependence it is useful to rationally process what is happening.

- Strengthens self-esteem: Low self-esteem is one of the main causes of emotional dependence. Without this element, we would not sacrifice all our independence and freedom to follow another person. To improve self-esteem, the best solution is to ask a therapist for help in order to investigate the causes of the disorder.

- Learn to be alone and rediscover emotional, psychological and physical independence: you cannot be good with others if you are not good with yourself first. If you do not know how to enjoy the time when you are alone, it will be difficult to have a mature relationship with others. It is normal to want a partner or friends but it is not healthy to feel the urgent need or to be dependent on this idea. Dedicate yourself to new hobbies and use your free time for yourself. Little by little you will be able to open yourself up to others and establish healthy, mature relationships.

These steps can set the stage for you to rethink and redesign your relationships and start to get out of emotional dependence.

Exercises to get out of emotional addiction

In this paragraph we will present some exercises to get out of emotional dependence, to be able to say:

"I am cured of emotional dependence"

In the previous paragraph we emphasized that the first step to get out of emotional dependence is to accept the problem. Once the problem has emerged, we can use some exercises that can help us to overcome this moment (although of course the main advice is always to turn to a specialist who can accompany us on our journey):

- ➤ Concentrate on the present moment: spend 10 minutes a day doing something you love by focusing mainly on the senses and packing your thoughts that have nothing to do with this moment.
- ➤ Focus on yourself: learn to say no and do only what you want to do, without getting dragged into the commitments, goals and thoughts of others. Start with the small things and then involve the whole reality
- ➤ To affirm: that is, to take the living space that we are entitled to, making others respect our limits (and obviously respecting theirs).
- ➤ Eliminate the sense of guilt. Very often addiction creates non-existent guilt: writing in a list all the moments that make us feel guilty can help us to resize and understand our sense of guilt.
- ➤ Learn how to manage shame: we can't please everyone and we can make mistakes. We learn to manage this kind of feeling, starting with muscle relaxation exercises.
- ➤ Make room for your passions: Be autonomous and free to choose.
- ➤ Living the mourning, separations and painful feelings. Processing the detachment and separations can take past relationships to their rightful place, thus accepting that the pain exists but without feeding it.
- ➤ Accept and discover one's true beauty.

These reflections and exercises to get out of emotional dependence, can help us in everyday life to try to find a balance.

If you still have doubts, do not be afraid to ask for help or contact a specialist.

Care for Emotional Addiction

Treatment for emotional dependency may vary depending on the severity of the dependency.

As mentioned at the beginning of the chapter, emotional dependence is not considered a real mental disorder, but a behavior disorder that can occur in several pathological personality disorders, such as borderline or personality disorder, associated with another range of symptoms.

Treatment for emotional addiction is based on a therapy that takes two forms:

- ➢ a short-term therapy to help the patient in his or her current suffering
- ➢ A long-term therapy that leads the patient to resolve situations of physical and emotional neglect, abandonment or mistreatment that undermine self-esteem and self-image and thus lead the person to the search for a relationship in which he or she feels loved and respected. The point is not to not depend on anyone but to create a healthy relationship based on love and respect and not on pathological behavior.

If you want to receive more information on the subject and if you think you need help, you can consult our list of professionals who are experts in the treatment of emotional dependence.

How to fight emotional addiction with therapy

To overcome emotional dependence and break away from a person we can use different types of therapy, we can also choose to choose individual or couples therapy.

In the case of individual therapy we will try to work on the typical resistances of emotional dependence, articulating the therapy to get out of the dependence in different stages. We will try to start from the most immediate problems that include the relationship, "abstinence" towards the partner and obsession with the partner. In a second phase we will try to study the family history and childhood trauma, and then we will reach a later phase where we will try to strengthen self-esteem and try to help the patient to regain possession of his life.

The therapy, however, could also include a couple therapy to assess the emotional co-dependence and try to loosen the symbiotic control so that the two co-dependent figures can regain possession of their own identity. In this sense we will work on several points including trying to loosen the control over the partner, find a more solid balance and live the separation in a non-obsessive way.

To get out of emotional and affective dependence, you need time and professional support: these exercises to overcome emotional dependence combined with therapy can help you identify and fight this disorder.

CHAPTER 10 • Fear of Abandonment

The fear of abandonment cannot be defined as a real disorder, but it can still lead to some addictions, such as emotional and emotional dependence, and to live badly love or friendship stories because the fear of losing the other always becomes predominant compared to the relationship itself.

In psychology, the abandonment syndrome is linked to an excessive and overwhelming concern about the possible estrangement and abandonment of people close to each other.

Fear stems from thoughts and concerns about the abandonment of a loved one and can be caused by inadequate physical and emotional care during childhood.

If you had a parent who abandoned the family when you were a child, you could see for yourself what it means: it affects the whole family, mother and children and jeopardizes the balance of the house.

It can also make it difficult for the child to trust adults and make them worry about who will be the next person to abandon them.

You will probably be asked a question:

If you are unable to form a relationship of trust with someone, how will you know they will not abandon you?

That's right, you can't.

And that will lead you to feel unable to be loved, to have this fear of being abandoned and to fear spending the rest of your life alone.

Many people grow up with this fear.

Some of them are consistently affected throughout their lives: they are worried about being rejected by peers, partners and social circles in general.

For others, these fears are not fully realized until they enter into romantic relationships.

If you suffer from abandonment syndrome, it can be very difficult for you to maintain healthy relationships. This paralyzing fear can lead you to create a wall to avoid being hurt or to unconsciously sabotage the relationship.

Things may go well for a while, but at some point, you feel awash with insecurities and thoughts about your partner leaving.

Although not officially a phobia, it is undoubtedly one of the most common and dangerous fears of all: there are compulsive behaviors and thought patterns that affect relationships and often result in real abandonment and estrangement.

The first step to solve it is to recognize and understand it.

Understand why you feel this way.

So let's go ahead and explore its causes, symptoms and long-term effects so that we can understand when it is good to ask for help.

Causes

Several causes can explain the presence of this fear.

As children, for example, individuals can experience real loss, rejection or trauma that can cause insecurity and lack of confidence in the world. These losses and traumas can be dramatic, such as the death of a loved one, neglect or emotional and physical abuse.

To feel safe, children need to be seen, understood and cared for, especially when they are angry.

Exploring attachment patterns can offer people some clues about their fear of rejection and being abandoned. Understanding how parents have related and whether or not they have experienced a safe attachment can give people some insight into their relationships in the present.

Safe attachment is formed when parents are consistently available and attuned to the child's needs.

Difficulties and developmental breaks can lead children to form unsafe attachments: this can lead them to cling to the parent in an attempt to meet their needs, but constantly struggle to see them satisfied.

Insecure attachment leads children to be often anxious and have to deal with an ambivalent parent: sometimes it is helpful and loving, sometimes it is rejecting or overly intrusive.

Some signs that the child may have abandonment issues are:

- ➤ Anxiety of separation
- ➤ Concern or panic
- ➤ Fear of being alone
- ➤ Get sick often due to stress
- ➤ Difficulty concentrating.

One way to help them is to reassure them about your love and their role in your life. Parents may also find it helpful to let children know what their daily "plan" is.

Knowing what to expect can help children feel reassured about the presence of their parents. And it can make them feel safer even when the parent is not present.

Some children experience what is called "child abandonment syndrome. This can occur after the death or physical or emotional abandonment of the parent. Symptoms can range from isolation, low self-esteem to eating disorders or addictions.

If not identified early, these symptoms can become severe and make it very difficult to form relationships or live a peaceful life.

Disorders in which the fear of abandonment manifests itself

There are some personality disorders in which this fear is typical and frequent.

Avoiding personality disorder

This personality disorder (other than Social Phobia) involves the fear of being abandoned and the feeling of feeling socially inhibited or inadequate.

Borderline personality disorder

Also in this personality disorder the fear of abandonment plays a fundamental role. Many individuals with this disorder show that they have been physically and/or sexually abused as children or have lived in a highly confrontational family atmosphere.

Separation anxiety disorder

If a child does not overcome separation anxiety and it interferes with daily activities, he or she may develop separation anxiety disorder.

Signs and symptoms of this disorder include:

- panic attacks
- anguish at the mere thought of being separated from loved ones
- refusal to leave home without a parent or to be left home alone
- nightmares related to being separated from loved ones
- physical problems, such as stomach or headaches, when you are separated from loved ones.

In addition, adults can also suffer from this disorder.

Symptoms of Abandonment

The symptoms of the abandonment syndrome are quite recognizable, because they are almost always defined within the relationship itself and are symptoms characterized by an irrational fear of losing the other.

We can classify in these symptoms both on a psychological and physical level:

- Feelings of anxiety related to separation
- Low self-esteem and feel unworthy of being loved
- Lack of trust in others
- Insecurity and difficulty in accepting criticism
- Difficulty in being oneself in a relationship and creating emotional intimacy
- Living toxic and extreme situations in order not to separate from a relationship
- Dysfunctional and unbalanced relational schemes
- Emotional instability, which can lead to anger and fear
- Inability to have long term relationships (but yes short term)
- Get attached to people quickly but also quickly forget them
- Don't be yourself and please the other person
- Blame yourself if things don't work out.
- Tend to stay in the relationship even realizing that it is not healthy.

All these symptoms are typical of people who suffer from fear of abandonment and do not have to occur within a relationship, but they can also involve family, friends or relationships in general.

The symptoms are normally related to insecurity, fear of losing the other and not feeling loved, normally leading people to an emotional dependent relationship.

Let's take a closer look at the different cases.

Fear of being left

The fear of abandonment can be concretized in the fear of being left by one's partner. This can also happen within marriage or cohabitation causing very intense separation anxiety.

For the person who suffers from such fear, being left is a fact that will inevitably happen sooner or later. But not because it really is so, but the feeling is to be always on the edge of a precipice, where the partner can leave or betray at any time.

Obviously, these relationships are lacking in trust and very often lead to make the prophecy of being left real, as the relationship becomes unbearable.

Despite this, however, the person who suffers from abandonment syndrome cannot objectively reason about his or her responsibility to be left by the partner (i.e. that obsessive, jealous, melodramatic and controlling behaviors can cause a relationship to end), but will attribute the end of the relationship to that it cannot be loved and is always abandoned by everyone.

Fear of losing someone

The fear of abandonment is not only about relationships, who has lost a loved one during childhood, can develop a feeling of anxiety for fear of losing a person with whom he is living a relationship, whether professional, love or friendship.

In short, fear could influence any healthy relationship. In particular, the fear of losing a person concerns both the possibility that this person will no longer form part of their life, but also the thought that this person may die or something may happen to them.

Fear of being abandoned in children

The fear of being abandoned is a fear that comes from attachment patterns.

These attachment patterns are basically behavioral, relational and affective patterns that parents teach their children and are a reflection of their relationship. Children will treat themselves and others according to these attachment patterns in which they have been involved.

So if there is difficulty, separation or abandonment these affective patterns may suffer a dysfunction and create a pattern of attachment that could lead to insecurity, low self-esteem, dependence and fear of abandonment.

In fact, adults who have suffered from abandonment as children will tend to feel insecure and develop relationships where they are afraid of rejection and anticipate it or obsessively look for signs of disinterest in their partner.

The result will be possessive relationships, full of jealousy and attempts at control, without trust and mostly melodramatic.

Now let's see how this fear can influence relationships in a decisive way and then go directly to the practical part.

How does the abandonment syndrome manifest itself in relationships?

An individual's history of early attachment acts as an internal working model for how he expects relationships to work (Attachment Theory).

This means that people can bring their insecurities and expectations about how others will behave from childhood to adulthood.

If you experience an ambivalent pattern as a child, this will develop into a concerned attachment as an adult, in which you continue to feel strongly insecure in your relationships.

Adults who experience abandonment syndrome often have this style of attachment: they tend to anticipate rejection and look for signs of disinterest in their partner.

Their fears can also be triggered by very subtle or imaginary signs of rejection based on the real rejection they experienced in childhood.

As a result, they may act possessive, controlling, jealous as well as showing behaviors such as need for reassurance and lack of trust. Often, they believe that unless they express their anxiety and anger dramatically the other will hardly respond to them.

Other times fears can instead lead to suppress their feelings completely.

In both cases, these individuals are extremely influenced in the present by events from their past.

Resolving these emotions is the key to feeling more secure and living healthier relationships.

How this fear impacts relationships

This fear manifests itself in ways in which the individual firmly believes that the partner will leave him/her. It is not a question of if it will happen, but of when.

This leads her to spend every day worrying about being abandoned, accusing her partner of betrayal or wanting to leave.

These individuals feel they are incapable of trust, because trust has been completely broken in the past. This leads them to recreate relationships of the same kind: the self-fulfilling prophecy.

Despite this, these people never take responsibility and fail to understand their contribution to the ultimate death of their relationship.

Their most frequent interpretation is that "they cannot be loved and that others always abandon them without explanation".

A TYPICAL EXAMPLE

To better explain how individuals with this syndrome can deal with a relationship, I would like to give a typical example of how the relationship begins and evolves.

1) The Knowledge of the Other

At this stage you feel relatively safe. Not being emotionally involved yet, you can continue to live life quietly.

2) The Honeymoon phases

In this phase the choice to commit is made. You begin to spend a great deal of time with each other, to feel good and secure.

3) The Real Relationship

The honeymoon phase cannot last forever. Sooner or later real life manifests itself: people can get sick, have family problems, work changes, etc.

This phase of the relationship can be terrifying for those who suffer from fear of abandonment, because it may indicate that the other is moving away.

4) The Light Detachment Phase

People are human and can have emotions and thoughts of various kinds. Beyond how much they may care about someone, it would be unhealthy to expect them to always think only of that person.

After the honeymoon phase, it is perfectly normal for there to be a slight detachment: this can take the form of a non-response to a message, a missed call or a few days on your own.

5) The Reaction

For those who are afraid of being abandoned, this is a turning point. In fact, he will tend to interpret that slight detachment as a real estrangement.

Some people react by becoming very needy, looking for proof of the love of the other, others instead refuse before being rejected (Fear of Loving).

Still others think that that slight detachment is due to them try to turn into the "perfect partner" so as to prevent abandonment.

In a healthy relationship, the individual is able to understand the situation for what it is: the slight detachment is a natural phase that has nothing to do with him.

6) The partner's point of view

From the partner's point of view, the change of personality seems to emerge from nothing: those who do not suffer from this fear do not understand what is really happening.

Just as it happens in phobias, it is impossible to convince in words those who suffer from this fear.

Despite the many reassurances of the partner, nothing changes.

And these behaviors will eventually drive him away, leading to the very conclusion that you fear more.

The long-term effects of fear of abandonment

Suffering from this fear for a long time can lead to a number of long-term effects, among them:

- Intimate and non-intimate relational difficulties
- low self-esteem
- inability to trust others
- anger problems
- mood swings
- emotional dependence
- fear of intimacy
- anxiety disorders
- panic attacks
- depressive disorders

It is therefore important to try to recognize it quickly and find valid and effective methods to overcome it before it is too late.

How to overcome the abandonment syndrome

Fortunately, attachment patterns are not fixed.

As adults, we can develop secure patterns in many ways.

Obviously, one cannot expect one's partner to fill the gaps or heal all the wounds of our childhood, but experiencing a secure attachment can offer us a new relational model in adulthood.

Attachment research has shown that it is not only what happens to individuals during childhood that influences adult relationships, but it is also how much they have been able to make sense of what they have experienced by feeling all the emotions involved.

If an individual is able to form a relationship with those who have experienced a secure attachment, they can learn that there is no need to desperately cling to each other to satisfy their personal needs.

One of the most effective ways to develop security is through therapy: experiencing a secure relationship with the therapist can help the person form a secure attachment.

As human beings we are not victims of our past, but we need to deal with it to create a better future.

When you can make sense of your past you can feel much less that intense fear of being abandoned. And even when you feel it, you are better able to calm down, manage and overcome it. You can also improve and strengthen your relationships instead of reacting with fear and insecurity.

The 7 steps to face the fear of abandonment

As we have seen, many people have this fear because they were abandoned very early. Sometimes it is a previous relationship, but in most cases the cause is to be found in childhood.

I want to give you some steps to overcome and manage this fear so that you can conduct healthier and more satisfying relationships.

1) <u>Recognize that you are worthy of love</u>

The emotional battle underneath those suffering from abandonment syndrome is linked to the feeling of not being worthy of love.

Has it ever happened to you to feel this way?

Since the person who had to take care of you has abandoned you, this has led you to have the conviction that you are neither loved nor lovable. The child's brain elaborates something like this: "if he had loved me, he would not have abandoned me".

Over time you may have begun to wonder why:

- "Wasn't I cute enough?"
- "Was I not smart enough?"
- "Was I not good enough?"

These thoughts can become very deep and continue into adulthood: the result is an adult who feels undeserving of love.

Here the first step to overcome this fear is to recognize that you are worthy of love and become emotionally self-sufficient.

Your identity should never be linked to a relationship:

- ✓ It's a part of you but it doesn't define you.
- ✓ It's okay if you are single or alone.
- ✓ Do not base your value on something external to you.
- ✓ You are worthy of love simply because you are yourself. That's all you need.

Therapy can be very useful to develop this emotional self-sufficiency of yours: it is not a process that happens instantly but reminding yourself every day that you are responsible for your emotions and that you are an individual with your own needs and desires.

2) If you want to manage your fear, understand it

Try asking yourself some questions:

> Where does your fear of abandonment begin?
>
> What happened in your life that made you feel this way?
>
> Are your past fears manifesting in your current relationships?

Questions like these can help you understand when and where your fear started and how it is still affecting you today.

3) Accept that a certain level of fear can always remain

Being afraid is human: you may not be able to eliminate it completely, but you can absolutely have more control over it.

It is essential to recognize when these moments occur in your relationships: identifying dysfunctional patterns can reveal where the deepest cause of fear itself is hidden.

4) Stop giving responsibility to your partner for these fears

To overcome the fear of abandonment you need to look inside. If you continue to give responsibility to others you will never be able to really deal with it.

Concretely, this means stopping controlling behavior and following every fear-based thought.

Obviously, it's easier said than done.

That's why the figure of the therapist can be of great help.

5) Accept the idea to be alone

Being alone is ok. You don't need another person in your life to be valuable.

It's okay to be single as well as in a relationship.

If your relationship ends, you have the opportunity to embrace your loneliness and understand the feelings and emotions that emerge from it.

Both being single and, in a relationship, has both positive and negative aspects.

6) Surround yourself with people who accept you for who you are

No one can solve all your problems or meet all your needs. A solid group of friends plays an extremely important role in our lives.

Many people who suffer from abandonment syndrome feel that they have never had a real group to refer to. For whatever reason, they have always felt disconnected from others.

Whatever stage of your life, it is important to surround yourself with people who can accept you for who you are.

You can begin your search by making a list of what you like, of your passions.

The next step is to actively seek out who shares your interests.

7) Stop chasing the emotionally unavailable

Some people with this fear seek relationships with people who are elusive and emotionally unavailable.

If you are one of them, it is important to break the cycle and look for partners who are ready to have a relationship with you. Don't settle for someone who can only give you 50%.

You deserve to have a relationship that satisfies you 100%.

CHAPTER 11 •   What is Jealousy

Jealousy can be considered a normal feeling, turned towards the other; it is that feeling of exclusivity of the relationship with the other person that implies dislike, suspicion or hostility towards third people seen as potential or current competitors.

For jealousy to break out, a simple and pure feeling of exclusivity is not enough, but the other must be perceived as an integral part of the jealous.

The jealous must be able to have complete control over the body, mind and paradoxically also over his partner's dreams. It implies a particular form of establishing relationships with the other, since it is salient to investigate the dynamics and processes with which the jealous person relates to the partner and how jealousy can be experienced by both the subject and the partner who suffers it.

It is important to investigate the emotional experience of the jealous person, i.e. what he feels, how he feels it, for how long he feels it and how he experiences or suffocates this feeling that tears relationships apart.

Pathological jealousy is generated by behaviors that are not reflected in reality, by unfounded actions, and derives, basically, from an anguish that takes shape in the mind without any objective response. This anguish produces real mental representations in which the scenario, the rival and, more than anything else, the evidence of infidelity is built ad hoc.

What it means to be jealous

Being afraid of losing the exclusivity of the relationship and feeding on the pretence of being enough for the other.

Is it true that love means jealousy?

Is there a good jealousy and a bad jealousy?

Can jealousy make you lose your head?

So many questions, too many maybe, but the jealousy is also this: questions, doubts, insecurities, confusion.

Jealousy is a very special emotion. It manifests itself with a subtle anxiety that arises from the belly and goes up to the head, negatively affecting our thoughts.

In fact, jealousy is more related to the idea of possession than love. It expresses itself with variable intensity just when we feel a sense of threat (real or imaginary) for what we consider our property.

This is exactly how it is: those who are jealous are not afraid of losing love, but unconsciously pretend to fill all the affective needs of their partner with their presence. He does not accept his own limit of importance in the relationship.

Feeling jealousy is perhaps inevitable and it is not at all easy to establish the right amount. It is more useful to ask ourselves how we feel when we feel jealous and what effects our behavior has on the relationship and on the partner.

Here are some examples of behavior inspired by jealousy:

1) Checking your partner's cell phone;
2) Investigating in an attempt to find out where he is going or who he is meeting with;
3) you get nervous because you notice that for some time now you have adopted a new look or care more about the way you dress.

Then you imagine that you meet someone in secret and you are invaded by a series of obsessive negative thoughts and so on:

- you make phone calls;
- you send text messages, waiting for an answer that satisfies you;
- you check Facebook.

The balance is really precarious and all it takes is an answer that does not correspond to what one hopes and expects to reject oneself in the spiral of obsession.

Jealousy can become a real torment, and can compromise the relationship to the point of destroying it. If you cannot change the situation on your own then it is important to ask for external support and talk to someone who can help you evaluate the situation more objectively and eventually find the right balance.

Go to the root of the problem and opt for an individual path of psychotherapy, which helps to weaken certain mechanisms that govern excessive reactions of jealousy as scenes without a valid reason and absurd prohibitions of the type:

"I don't want you to talk to her anymore!

"If you say goodbye to him one more time, you're done with me!"

These kinds of things cause tension, dissatisfaction and conflict within the couple.

The risk is to pull the rope too much and, at a certain point, see the partner running away, because the jealousy has become suffocating.

It is also important to emphasize that obsessive and oppressive jealousy is a real torment even for those who feel it. A sort of sea monster with tentacles that wraps and immobilizes in a vice until it takes your breath away.

And here it is that, even if there are no valid and concrete reasons to be jealous, imagine them until you realize and believe them!

A real torment, especially when, despite trying, you realize that you cannot get rid of them.

The spiral of jealousy is fed by insecurities, lack of confidence in the partner, but above all in oneself. Here too we find, as in emotional dependence, the fear of being abandoned. Or rather, one could say that if one is present the other is almost certainly present too.

The key to everything is to return to believe in one's own possibilities and potential! If you have adequate confidence in yourself and your partner, you will not have many opportunities to feel jealous and when you do, it will be a useful experience to reflect on the relationship and assess whether there are concrete reasons to worry.

If you cannot change the situation on your own, then it is important to ask for help and opt for an individual path of psychotherapy, which helps to weaken certain mechanisms that govern excessive jealousy reactions.

CHAPTER 12 • Symptoms of Jealousy and How to Recognize Them

How many times in a single day do you think obsessively and wearily about a potential betrayal? If you think about it for more than an hour a day, then it means you may have a problem with pathological jealousy.

Obsessive thinking and control behaviors are the first symptoms of pathological jealousy.

- Can't you stop thinking about it?
- The only alternative you see is to act on control behaviors?
- Do you steal the phone to control chats?
- To see the calls he receives or makes? Check if you find in some pocket cards that can reveal the betrayal?
- Do you question every word he says, harass your partner with questions that create pressure to expose him?

Physical symptoms of pathological jealousy:

- Anxiety
- Depression
- Intense negative emotions
- Obsessive and sometimes aggressive behavior

Where does pathological jealousy take you?

To the loss of your partner. You cannot expect your relationship to be based on constant torment, on controls. Have you already come to take away your partner's freedom? Do you forbid them to go out with friends? Do you prevent him/her from making phone calls with them?

Have you already gone to his workplace to make scenes? To check who he does what with? When he comes home from work, do you give him the third degree?

Have you already done, or are you doing one or more of these actions?

- You hunt for meticulous, but non-existent clues, because you think the smallest detail is overwhelming evidence of a possible betrayal;
- You follow your partner everywhere; you've hired someone to follow him for you;
- Check clothes, wallets, bags, drawers, cabinets, the car
- Keep your cell phone, pc, tablet, any means that can be a communication tool, because you are convinced that somewhere there is evidence of betrayal;
- You are obsessed with the certainty of betrayal. You torment your partner with your accusations, and his denials are for you the confirmation of his lies;
- You construct stories, which for you have a value of absolute truth, but which in reality have no practical subsistence.

If you are answering YES to this list of symptoms of pathological jealousy you can admit with yourself that you are a pathological jealous. And that your obsessive jealousy is ruining the life not only of your partner, but also of yourself.

To better understand the symptoms of pathological jealousy, I describe better its characteristics and what are the contents of the obsessions of pathological jealousy.

Obsessive thoughts about the existence of a rival lead the jealous to make really strange accusations. There are real delusions, which see the partner commit adultery, even when the victim is objectively at work or in other places, where other people can testify. The jealous person enters an endless circle that can also lead to extreme and dangerous actions. Unless the victim of pathological jealousy is able to break the relationship.

So, in any case, the symptoms of pathological jealousy lead to the breaking of the bond creating really and seriously a serious suffering to both partners: victim and executioner.

- ➤ The 4 Types of jealousy: help to identify the symptoms of pathological jealousy
- ➤ Depressive jealousy: you don't feel up to the partner;
- ➤ Obsessive jealousy: you are constantly gripped by doubt as to whether or not you are loved;
- ➤ Anxious Jealousy: you live with the nightmare of being left;
- ➤ Paranoid Jealousy: characterized by constant and excessive suspicion.

Symptoms of Pathological Jealousy

At the base of the problem we can hypothesize anxiety and low self-esteem, the shy pathological person is a person who dislikes himself little, and tries to hide this insecurity with very strong behaviors, even aggressive, up to extreme gestures. There may be other problems such as personality disorder, or emotional addiction. Definitely a picture articulated on several points.

<u>Are males or females more jealous?</u>

In "balanced" jealousy, not pathological, in the couple is stimulating because it brings attention back to the importance of the presence and exclusivity of the other, thus giving flavor to the relationship.

The intensity of jealousy felt is the same for males and females, are the behaviors that are different from men and women.

Men seem to prefer more active behaviors in case of betrayal of their partner: they face the problem, also looking for the rival.

While women suffer more emotionally, they tend not to expose the partner because it would be too painful. It is possible that some women develop guilt feelings, and blame them for the betrayal acted by their partner.

The most common reaction to both sexes is to brood tormentedly over what happened, and this happens with equivalent frequency, duration and intensity in both sexes.

In pathological jealousy, it seems that among women, there is the highest rate of depressive and obsessive jealousy, while among males it is the most worrying form of paranoid jealousy.

What are the causes of pathological jealousy?

Pathological jealousy, in all probability, is the expression of Dysfunctional Adaptive Maladaptive Schemes that have been produced by the invalidation of early essential needs due to emotional deficiencies of the family environment, in particular the theoretical framework elaborated by the Therapy Scheme (Young, Klosko, Weishaar) allows us to understand how the frustration of particular needs can be the cause of obsessive jealousy. Here we will focus only on two domains that, however, in my opinion, represent the core of insecurity, inadequacy and lack of amiability that are very often present in the subject who manifests obsessive jealousy:

1) "Abandonment / Instability". The presence of this early dysfunctional pattern feeds the belief that the people in charge of our care/protection will sooner or later abandon us or cease to meet our needs; this pattern is the result of a family environment in which one or both parents have been perceived as unreliable, not very present or following the abandonment or death of one parent or other caregiver.

2) "Emotional Deprivation". Those who present this pattern are convinced that their needs for care, affection, love, consolation

and acceptance will remain unsatisfied; this pattern is generated when the child, in a systematic and continuous manner, and deprived of the necessary care is, above all, the need to receive warmth, affection, consolation, validation of emotions, possibility to trust and receive help. Children who manifest this pattern have grown up in cold families that perhaps meet their concrete needs but, for various reasons, have been deprived of warmth, empathy, security of being loved, self-esteem; in many cases, one or both parents have had a critical or disqualifying attitude towards the child making him feel inadequate, lacking in quality, unlovable, generating the belief that others will never take care of him.

These patterns are repeated in the adult every time the opportunity to engage in an emotional relationship, he can even avoid venturing into love stories because he is convinced that no one cares and that sooner or later, when the partner will know him really well will abandon him, so there is no point in deluding yourself. In the pathological jealous often the pattern of abandonment and emotional deprivation are activated at the same time feeding the doubts that the partner will surely find, and only a matter of time, a more interesting object of love, he will then be abandoned confirming the painful belief that he does not have the qualities to be loved. The individual who shows obsessive jealousy towards the partner often has low self-esteem, insecurity, feels inadequate and lacking in quality, these experiences explain the control behaviors aimed at preventing a scenario considered unlivable.

<u>How to get out of pathological jealousy</u>

You can fight symptoms of pathological jealousy. It is very useful to talk about it, ask for help right away. Let yourself be helped to rebuild your sense of personal security and become stronger. And trigger positive change.

When pathological jealousy takes on the characteristics described above, it is advisable to use a therapy that can recognize and break down the dysfunctional patterns underlying the insecurity towards the partner; these patterns are the result of systematic and continuous experiences of emotional invalidation. Generally, unless the person undertakes a path of psychotherapy, the person is unaware of the presence of these patterns and "justifies" the obsessive jealousy as a trait of his personality "I'm like that", even when he takes note of the existence of these patterns is not able to change them alone, they are resistant to change because they are engraved in the deepest layers of the soul.

A valid cure for pathological jealousy is represented by Cognitive Behavioral Psychotherapy and in particular the approach of Schema Therapy, specifically developed to recognize and demolish dysfunctional personality patterns.

CHAPTER 13 • How to Overcome Jealousy

In this chapter I want to show you 7 ways to overcome jealousy by buying back the car control.

1) It may seem trivial, but how about starting to believe your partner?

Yes, take his word for it. Trust is the basis of every relationship. It is very offensive to your partner that you always doubt his word or the intentions of his behavior. Constant questioning can be very destructive even in a long-lasting relationship.

You may sometimes mistrust your partner, but it is important to find the strength to act as if you believe him. If you have been able to verify that he was really where he said he was, stop doing it and start giving in to the feelings he shows you.

2) Easier said than done, but stop comparing yourself to others.

For some (not all) jealousy depends on low self-esteem. "How can you love me? I don't understand how someone can be attracted to someone like me!".

We should avoid asking ourselves why someone loves us. If he or she loves you, it depends on an indefinable quality that you possess that cannot be explained. So stop trying to 'understand' why you can like him or her.

3) It might be a terrible thought, but be ready to accept it.

Even people with high self-esteem can experience intense jealousy if they have a tendency to want to be the center of attention. People like this regard their partner as their property and tend not to want to share this 'property'. Such as letting the partner smile or socialize with another person. They behave a bit like a spoiled child.

But people are not objecting or toys that need to be constantly monitored. If you want to love someone properly, you have to be willing to lose them.

Anger, fear and jealousy drive away the love that needs a little bit of courage to grow up. You may be afraid of losing your loved one, but if you really want to use your imagination, think of the 'worst' that could happen and you will feel better.

Try writing 10 positive ways in which you would rebuild your new life if your relationship ended. Imagine how you could live without your partner.

Fear is definitely stronger when we feel we have no other options, so avoid basing your whole life on one person.

4) Don't play with feelings.

Jealousy is terribly uncomfortable. People sometimes behave in a way that makes their partner jealous in order to feel better. Avoid doing so. Flirting with other men or women in front of your partner, saying how attractive, funny, funny a colleague or friend is; or talking about past lovers only helps humiliate you.

5) Avoid confusing fantasy with reality.

Jealousy often comes from a destructive use of fantasy. Therefore, avoid listening too much to your imagination.

Think about it: Your partner comes home later than you thought. So you begin to imagine that he had an aperitif with that "beautiful" person who works in his office or with that other very sensual person you happened to see in the gym.

You are upset, upset, frightened - but you have no proof that what you imagined is real.

As soon as you get home, you react in a 'strange' way, very coldly or on the contrary you get angry and lose control. Your partner in turn gets defensive and gets angry.

When you feel very angry try to throw out your thoughts already, describing in detail what you imagine your partner is doing while he is out without you. It will help you rationalize.

When you stop being emotional just because you imagined something, take a step forward and try to regain control of your jealousy.

6) Loosen your grip.

If your partner wants to spend the weekend with his friends, let him go. Keeping him 'imprisoned' will only serve to build the desire to escape your possessiveness. Set him free (that doesn't mean you should let him go). If you go out together, let him talk to his attractive colleague (keep in mind that they may find their colleague less attractive than you imagine). If you suspect that he wants to make you jealous, short-circuit him by showing you relaxed.

7) Use your imagination to feel better, not worse.

Try this exercise: close your eyes and relax. Now think about the scenario that makes you more jealous. Imagine your partner outside with someone else? See him talking and laughing with someone else?

Now, breathe deeply and concentrate trying to relax the different parts of your body, imagine you are calm, relaxed, disinterested in this kind of situation. Visualize your partner doing all the things that make you jealous and watch yourself not responding with jealousy, but rather with serene detachment.

The more you can do this exercise, the less jealousy will make you lose control.

CHAPTER 14 • How to Build Trust in the Relationship

The happiest and most rewarding relationships are based on a very solid foundation of unconditional trust. If you want your relationship to reach its full potential, both you and your partner must learn how to create such trust. Most couples believe that trust is all about sexual fidelity, but although it is an important element, there is much more to work on.

Trust is an important issue. Trust is the foundation of free, uninhibited, generous, authentic love. It is also the basis of serene relationships in which each partner feels heard, supported, and feels that he or she can be himself or herself without fear of the other's judgment.

Respect values in the Relationship

Be faithful. If a member of the couple is not faithful, the relationship quickly becomes impossible to continue. Sometimes people are able to overcome a betrayal, but often need professional help to do so. Promise to be faithful and keep your commitment. If your relationship does not make you happy, seek help from a qualified therapist instead of seeking comfort in some escapade.

Being faithful to a person means being faithful on all levels. This implies both physical and emotional fidelity. Some people believe that establishing an intimate bond with someone else by simply spending time together is not harmful to the couple, but it's not; over time your relationship will certainly suffer.

Give your partner space and encourage mutual respect. Trust develops only in healthy and safe environments. Hurting each other, verbally or physically, or rejecting your partner, only triggers unnecessary fears that can jeopardize trust. Attempting to control your partner's every move demonstrates a significant lack of trust, so try not to cling to his or her presence in a possessive way. Obsessive behavior will only drive the other person away.

If your partner wants to spend time with friends, try to agree. In this regard, it is still legitimate to talk about which behaviors are acceptable and which are not. For example, if one member of the couple wants to go clubbing with friends, but the other has concerns about it, it will be essential to talk about it to prevent future problems or bad moods.

Sincerely love your partner as he or she is. You both need to know that you are loved for the people you are and not for other reasons, such as money, family, physical appearance or even fear of being alone. Make sure that your relationship is based on meaningful reasons.

Make sure that your relationship is at the top of your priorities. It is easy to take the other person's presence for granted and neglect it. Try not to exhaust all your energy by interacting with others or engaging in everyday activities. Keep clear what is important to you. If living a happy relationship is one of your main life goals, then make sure that your partner always stays at the top of your priority list.

Don't back down from the first difficulties. Misunderstandings, quarrels and arguments can happen. Make sure that a normal disagreement or outburst of anger does not force your partner to fear being abandoned. Make sure that you never threaten the other person to leave.

Demonstrate Confidence

Maintain your own routine. Many people believe that having a lot of fun and things to do allows you to have a fabulous relationship; basically, they try to plan something new all the time to surprise each other. Although, from time to time, it is pleasant to be surprised, stability and repetitiveness are two much more important aspects of a relationship. A monotonous couple's life may sound boring, but for things to work out in the long term you need to be predictable. Trust is based on predictability.

Demonstrate reliability. Trust is about knowing you can count on someone. You are certain that your partner has certain behaviors, no matter what the circumstances. This trust gives rise to a feeling of security. Make sure that your partner can always count on you.

If you say you'll be home by 5:00 a.m., be on time and remember to let us know if you're going to be late. Consistency is one of the key factors of trust. If you are late 4 times out of 5 without even bothering to tell them, you will show that you think your needs are far more important than your partner's needs. For a relationship to be a happy and fulfilling one, both parties must strive to live up to their commitments.

Say what you think. More than anyone else, your partner can read your facial expressions. When you lie, you try to hide your real feelings or avoid saying what is really on your mind, but the other person can see it and, in some cases, may even feel betrayed. Knowing that you can blindly trust the words of others and that every thought is expressed without fear, allows you to build a strong and valuable bond.

Be sincere. Don't keep anything hidden, you don't have to keep secrets from your partner. As you may already know, sooner or later, the truth always comes to light and the consequences of not being completely honest will destroy trust and ruin your relationship.

Express your feelings without reservation. Too many people hide their real needs from their partner. Don't expect the other person to guess how you feel or what you would like them to do for you. It is essential that you both respect this rule. The fact that only one of you will see your needs as being permanently satisfied may make you feel overwhelmed, while the other will suffer from excessive neglect. Neither scenario is desirable.

Learn to say no when necessary. Paying attention to your partner's needs and trying to meet them is certainly correct, but sometimes it is important to be able to say no. It is not always possible to do everything, and occasional rejection will only increase respect for you. In the long term, taking a stand and imposing yourself when necessary will help to increase mutual trust.

Have more Confidence in your Partner

Believe in the skills of your partner. Believing that he can't succeed in something means putting your trust in him at risk. In such a situation the best thing to do is to talk about it in an honest and loving way. Together you can find a constructive solution and keep your mutual trust solid.

Trust your partner. How do you think he can trust you if you in turn show that you do not trust him? Successful relationships are based on reciprocity and cannot exist without a mutual exchange of trust.

To achieve your goal, you will need to learn to put aside your vulnerability. Often the presence of trust is linked to our inner feelings. If you tend to be very insecure, you can jeopardize the soundness of your relationship. Remember that until the facts prove it is a mistake, your job is to have full confidence in the person you love.

Give yourself the benefit of the doubt. The tendency to expect the worst to happen in every situation is a clear indicator of a lack of trust. Just because he hasn't phoned you doesn't mean he's betraying you. Trusting a person means always being willing to give them the benefit of the doubt. Each person deserves the opportunity to explain themselves before the other draws their own conclusions, which otherwise would not be objective.

Do not touch his phone. Has one or both of you set a password to access your phone? If so, you may have problems trusting each other. Although privacy is important, your phone should not be as impregnable as a bank vault. When trust is real, both members of the couple respect each other's privacy while having free access to each other's information. Believing that the person calling your partner may be a threat to your relationship is a serious trust issue that needs to be addressed.

Set him/her free. Often, when trust is lacking, you feel the need to monitor every step the person takes and always know who they are with. You tend to be possessive and feel threatened by anyone. However, trust is based on relying fully on the other person and allowing them to act freely. Having faith in someone means having faith in ourselves as well, and allows us to nurture healthy and lasting relationships.

CHAPTER 15 • Couple Conflicts

Among the most common conflicts in modern couples stands out the lack of realism, a characteristic that the grandparents possessed. Love between two human beings is not the answer to everything, but the ground in which to learn to give, grow and become more human.

The most common conflicts in modern couples are very far from those of our grandparents. In just three or four decades, relationships have changed a lot. New sources of conflict have emerged as gender roles and family structures have undergone major transformations.

Currently there are a number of emotional demands that did not exist before. In the past, the roles of friends, spouses, lovers, partners, etc. were not as marked and fundamental.

Nowadays, however, the idea that the couple should be one together has been installed. This means having to be able to respond to emotional, sexual, social and even philosophical expectations. A commitment that can overwhelm anyone.

This is why the most common conflicts in modern couples are mainly related to limits. There is confusion about aspects such as the boundary between intimacy and independence, or between freedom and commitment.

There is also a strong demand for contentment and happiness that, of course, no one can satisfy. Some do not even realize that the problem lies in the demand itself and not in the couple.

The most common conflicts in Relationship

Lack of intimacy

There are many couples who go to the psychologist to expose a shared problem: that is, not feeling understood by their partner. In most cases, the work to be done is to improve communication.

It seems that many couples are currently afraid to expose their weaknesses to each other. They do not feel comfortable talking about their fears or weaknesses. Nor do they feel that the other person is able to understand them.

Trust is not cultivated and this limits the ability to engage in sincere and authentic dialogues. Intimacy goes into crisis.

Control

Although, in theory, there is much more equity in the roles of couples today, in practice it may not be so true. According to the psychologist María José Carranza, from the University of Barcelona, very rigid patterns are currently maintained in the couple. They lead to inequality and resentment.

Among the most common conflicts in modern couples is the assumption of absolute control of the most important aspects of couple life by a member. One makes the decisions and the other follows him/her. Or, one protects and the other allows himself to be protected.

This is why it is common for one of the two to diminish themselves to the point of depression, without even trying to change the dynamic of the bond.

Differentiation

The differentiation concerns the process of separation from the family of origin. In ancient times, the principle prevailed: "Between wife and husband do not put the finger". Although there was a strong bond with the extended family, it was clear to everyone that the new couple that had joined needed independence and some distance.

Today it is no longer so clear. Often there is too much intrusive participation of the original family in the formation and destiny of a couple. Siblings meddle, grandparents end up raising nephews, uncles help out, etc.

In practice, there is no real differentiation from the family of origin and this is one of the most common conflicts nowadays.

Affection

Many people reach adulthood without having processed their attachment problems. No one has a perfect childhood and there are very few who do not carry the signs of this stage.

It may be that we have been cared for too much, in other cases we carry with us the trauma of our parents' divorce or the consequences of an absent father, etc. The possibilities are many.

The truth is that each of us should work on these gaps or latent traces to balance our emotions, expectations and renunciations. But, since this does not happen, the couple often ends up being the object into which all these inconsistencies are projected. And this becomes a source of confusion for both.

Definition of commitment

One of the most common conflicts in modern couples. Some people date and have sex regularly, but do not call themselves engaged. Others have been together for years, have children, but are only engaged and each life at home.

Then there are those who get married, divorce, but continue to have casual sex with each other.

Defining what commitment exists between two people has become a very difficult task. For many, the problem is the very definition of commitment. They claim that order and labels turn the relationship into a threat to freedom.

The most common conflicts in modern couples also have consequences. Many couples stop being such. Love understood in the most traditional way in many cases is rejected, when not hated.

In this way, some people seek the commitment of the other, the security of relying on the partner, while avoiding establishing a bond that corresponds to this feeling.

CHAPTER 16 • Overcoming the Crisis and Saving a Couple's Relationship

When two people decide to start a stable couple relationship, they normally do so because they rationally think they have a person next to them who deserves their interest and attention. That's not all: the two partners feel mutual feelings of affection and a series of positive emotions, resulting from being close and interacting. All this, not only the irrational part of emotions and feelings, is called love.

Love, in fact, is a feeling of living affection towards a person, which manifests itself as a desire to procure his good and seek companionship.

Today there is no longer any reason why two people, at least in the Western world, should join together, if not for love: there are no more family choices to satisfy, marriages arranged for reasons of interest or power, reparatory marriages after the loss of virginity. You get married, or you start living together, just because you feel good together, you love each other, you want to share your life experiences and, almost always, also because you have a plan to bring children into the world, to feel more complete and more fulfilled.

When you start a stable relationship, the last thought that might come to mind for the two partners is that of having to face one day a crisis or a separation, as well as being able to get to hate each other ferociously, so much so as to feel good only in the absence of the ex-lover.

With many chances instead, one day the crisis will knock on the door. It is natural to feel anxiety and sadness in this situation, as well as feelings of emptiness or loss.

The idea that something once held so much has shattered, or is shattering before one's eyes, can only generate a feeling of failure for the past and a lack of balance and perspectives, with respect to the present or the future.

The word "crisis", after all, comes from the Greek Krísis (from kríno = I judge) and means choice, judgment, separation. When there is a crisis it means that the time has come for judgment, choices, change: everything that was before can no longer exist, unless it is transformed, adapted to the new demands of reality.

In a couple's relationship the crisis can come as a result of betrayal, because of too much stress, because the two partners have evolved differently and now, they no longer recognize each other for what they were, for the constant quarrels, for changes in lifestyle, or for the birth of a child. The crisis brings with it the loss of homeostasis and a search for change; it is always a period of transition, which tends towards a new stability, as in the final break, or the choice to try a reconciliation.

Obviously then, after a crisis, reconciling does not mean simply starting over, everything as before: if there was a crisis it is precisely because that "as before" did not work, generated malaise, quarrels, misunderstandings, loss of interest in the partner, and the crisis came to demand a change.

If you have the impression that your relationship is falling apart and you want to save it, the first step will be self-analysis.

As mentioned so far, all couples go through a series of phases during their relationship. But while in some it is possible to proceed towards improvement, in others there seems to be a continuous lack of agreement and harmony. So much so that they find themselves in conflict about everything, even nonsense. Do you feel this way? Do you not know how to save the relationship?

With patience, love and a good disposition, you can overcome great obstacles. In this chapter we will discuss in detail some steps to save the relationship.

What to do to save the relationship?

Self-Analysis

It is almost impossible to solve a problem when you are not aware that you have it. The first step is therefore to become aware of the situation and look for the cause of disharmony.

In this sense, the best place to find the mistakes is within us. Analyse your behavior, your responses, the tone of your voice, the way you show affection and, above all, your feelings.

Keep in mind that if you lack the will to take your share of the blame in conflicts, the situation is unlikely to change. Self-observation is therefore essential. Taking a critical look at yourself, knowing how to observe yourself, allows you to be more empathetic and assertive with your partner.

What was not working in the relationship? What didn't work? What worked well? Once you have clarified these points, you need to start again from what worked well, despite everything. This is obviously the main glue of the couple, the one that more than anything else must be taken care of and valued. Then there is what worked little and what didn't work at all: here the changes required to the couple are really very deep and it is always a good idea to try to get help from a therapist, who can facilitate the change, solving the small objections or reluctance between the two partners, also because we must not forget the estrangement and the return to a selfish and narcissistic thinking that the crisis may have caused in both partners.

Conversation

Problems cannot be solved if they are not named. And for dialogue it is essential to keep a calm tone. If you adopt a defensive attitude, with a tone of reproach and full of resentment, you will never reach an agreement.

It is also necessary not to hurt yourself with words. If you are going to say something, it is best not to hurt or hurt your partner. Never disrespect.

Sometimes kindness is reserved for strangers, while with family members or partners it is always natural: it is a wrong concept. In fact, being polite and kind does not mean being false or constructed; on the contrary, it means deciding that you want to exercise dominion over yourself in order to show your partner your interest and respect. It should not be forgotten that sometimes the lack of interest towards the partner does not arise from striking facts, but can be generated simply by the established habit of feeling rude, or cold and detached, or even frankly rude and violent. In addition to this, one must also learn a healthy way of quarrelling, which is one in which the two partners say things clearly, but without ever taking offence. It is a difficult game of balance, but you can learn.

How to Improve Communication Quality

Try to base communication on calm and mutual respect. It's not easy to have a discussion with your partner about the problems and difficulties of the relationship without some style drop and without getting emotional.

Tackling the conversation politely and with due respect to the other person will show that you are committed to making this relationship work. Avoid swearing or raising your voice while discussing your problems with your partner. Rather, try to speak honestly and clearly about your feelings with a kind and loving attitude.

Before talking with your partner, apply relaxation techniques to stimulate the body to calm the mind. Breathing deeply, meditating or even practicing exercise before engaging in conversation are methods that will help you maintain the right balance.

Expose your feelings with honesty and precision.

To improve communication with your partner, it is important to strive to avoid possible misunderstandings or misunderstandings. To this end, try to speak frankly, sincerely and accurately about your feelings and wishes. If you believe that your partner is neglecting your relationship, you should explain honestly and transparently how and why this hurts you.

You could simply use these words: "I feel like I haven't spent a lot of time with you lately and I miss being with you, alone. You could then suggest going out to dinner to spend a romantic evening with you. At this point, your intentions will be clear and you will show that you are actually trying to communicate.

Also, during an argument, try to focus on what made you angry at that exact moment, rather than bringing up all your problems. If you plan to spend little time with your partner, focus the discussion on what you need to do to make time for yourself. If the topic of the argument is domestic chores, such as taking out the trash, focus on why it is important that you both do it.

Don't let the garbage discussion turn into a rebuke about your indifference to household chores or a criticism of your laziness and irresponsibility. Dealing with one issue at a time will help you not to be overwhelmed by problems and turn a simple discussion into a heated argument.

Learn to listen. Active listening involves being able to listen and respond to an interlocutor to improve mutual understanding. Instead of thinking of conversations as competitions or battles to be won, consider them as opportunities to learn more about each other. In this way, you will show that you see dialogue with your partner as a way to listen attentively, rather than attacking or ignoring his or her statements.

To listen actively, you need to focus your attention on the other person and wait for the end of their conversation without ever interrupting them. You must then be able to repeat what he said with your words. Even if you do not need to share his or her statements, this way you will still show that you understand his or her position and that you want to discuss his or her ideas by exchanging thoughts and emotions in a balanced way, rather than arguing.

Try to accept your partner's point of view. Active listening is only one aspect of effective communication. The other component is to give credit to the other's point of view, consider their feelings and discuss possible strategies to resolve the conflict. It could be an open discussion in which both of you propose interventions to adjust your routine and schedules to the needs of the couple or a personal proposal to resolve the conflict to be evaluated together. The important thing is to show that you have respect for the point of view of others and want to work together to find plausible solutions to the problem.

For example, your partner may complain that you stay in the office after hours and always come home late in the evening. Wait until it's over, then say: "I understand that you would rather see me come home early and not work late to spend more time with me. I also want to spend more time with you. Unfortunately, I won't be able to get out early until the day an important project is delivered, but I'll take you out to dinner this weekend so we can spend an evening together". This response shows that you have accepted his thinking and proposed a way to resolve the conflict. You are taking responsibility for your actions and showing understanding for your partner's point of view.

Respect times and distances

If two birds fly too close together, they may bother each other with wings. This metaphor means that you have to respect the time and space of your partner. Keeping it under control or under scrutiny is not healthy for anyone.

Respect the moments to spend alone (both your own and your partner's) and get used to doing some activities separately. This space will give oxygen to the relationship and renew the desire to meet again, unlike when you force the other to be together all the time.

Not all desires, of course, can be granted: for example, some may be absolutely contrary to your own values. In this case it is necessary to seek mediation, also through the search for new solutions for old problems. Again, the therapist's mediation work could be valuable.

Learn to trust to save the relationship

Trust is one of the fundamental pillars of every couple. Without trust we cannot live together, but we cannot claim it if we are not the first to give it.

If the relationship is falling apart, learning to trust, to listen, to put ourselves in each other's shoes is fundamental. You should not give in to attacks of jealousy and, in any case, you should choose to talk about it very calmly and affectionately.

Set new rules and limits

If there are clear rules to be respected, neither partner can claim to have misinterpreted the other's wish. Likewise, in the presence of unpleasant behavior, one can be better prepared to tolerate it, knowing that certain limits can never be exceeded.

Forgive

If the crisis was generated by the wrong behavior of one of the two partners, the one who was wronged should not feel automatically absolved of all responsibility: if there was a crisis, evidently not realizing in time the other's malaise, or underestimating it, may also have been a mistake. More rightly, the partner who caused the crisis, perhaps through betrayal, must show sincerely sorry behavior and create the conditions for the partner to return to trust. Whatever happened, the things to do to best overcome the crisis are these: analyze, understand, forgive, forget.

Try to do something special together

Those who live together experiences that produce positive emotions (joy, joy, interest, pride, empathy) tend to bond more. They don't necessarily have to be things out of the ordinary: in everyday life you can choose to do things, or hang out with people and situations, capable of transmitting pleasant and satisfying feelings to share.

Organize exclusive outings with your partner. One of the main reasons why couples go into crisis is that one of them starts to devote less and less time and energy to the relationship. Find moments to spend together by organizing outings and activities to share. Rediscover moments of intimacy where you can interact, chat, laugh and have fun.

A special evening in a nice restaurant or a mountain hike on your favorite trail are simple but effective ideas. Try to include activities that you both love and launch yourself and your partner into completely new adventures. This way the time spent together will be exciting and engaging for both of you.

Plan a romantic evening once a week. If you are both very busy with work and have many commitments, the ideal is to officially set a day of the week to spend together. Regardless of the work commitments that may come up, on that day you have to do something together, without anyone else. Having a weekly appointment will allow you to organize the evening in the best possible way and will give both of you the typical emotion of when you are waiting for a special moment.

Once you agree on the day, avoid missing the romantic date. In this way, you will show your partner your willingness to sacrifice any other commitment and keep your promise to be together.

Surprise your partner with a special evening. If you are trying to involve him more in your relationship and renew your commitment to each other, arrange a surprise date in an unusual place.

You could take your partner to a spa, go bowling or do some more extreme activities such as paintball or rafting. Think of something that reflects your partner's interests, but at the same time, can make him or her speechless.

Revitalize sexual desire

The discussions take us away from the partner on a sentimental level, but also on a physical level. When you argue or get angry, you lose the desire to be close and touch each other. The desire to kiss or create intimacy will take a back seat.

It is therefore important to resolve any small discussion immediately. Interrupt the tension, reaching an agreement to stop the avalanche of bad thoughts that lead to anger.

Having sex is essential to keep the flame of desire burning. Every moment can be nice to surprise your partner and make love.

Learn teamwork

Deciding to continue living together requires a renewed commitment to each other, a push, which this time can not only start from the heart, but can also be rational, to recreate an atmosphere of affection, solidarity, well-being. After all, if you have opted for reconciliation, you are obviously aware that, for your own well-being and your own values, living together with your partner, learning to play as a team, i.e. sharing good and bad luck, is definitely better than living a life in turmoil and uncertainty, where life satisfaction coincides with personal interest alone.

Follow the couple therapy

The vast majority of people try to hide that they have undertaken a course of couples therapy. Others refuse because they do not feel comfortable, showing their weaknesses seems inappropriate to them because they fear the judgment of others. But this thought is the premise of a resounding failure.

To turn to a professional to save the relationship can be very positive. It is advisable not to hesitate and make the necessary efforts. A psychologist will help to resolve outstanding issues with your partner.

A new beginning for the relationship

Do you remember when the relationship was going well? When did the problems start? To save the relationship, you need to go back in time and try to identify the triggers and factors that made the situation worse.

If you can find them together with your partner, it will be easier to find the solution together and try to love each other again. The ideal is to do this before it is too late, otherwise it will be impossible to find the lost feelings.

Both must want to save the relationship

Finally, there is an essential requirement to save a relationship that is falling apart: you have to really love each other and want both, not just a member of the couple.

You have to be honest with yourself and your partner. Because if the relationship does not work, it is better to talk about it clearly, close the door and wait for another opportunity.

CHAPTER 17 • Fear of Loving

This fear can be very sneaky because it does not allow you to enter into deep relationships and leads you to quickly move away just thinking about a more serious relationship.

"Why does loving scare me so much? It's something I can't avoid, but when I realize that I'm starting to fall in love I run away. I end the relationship and only then do I feel calm again. Otherwise I panic. And I can't stand it!"

Not facing it is tantamount to risking living a life of real emotional isolation, which can predispose to more serious disturbances.

That is why in this chapter I will try to deal with this topic in depth: I will explain what it is, how it manifests itself, the causes and as always, I will provide practical tools to work on you.

Philophobia (fear of love) is defined as a constant and apparently unjustified fear of falling in love, accompanied by anxious physical symptoms.

Consciously, those who suffer from it always have some good rational reason for their behavior: they are not made to be monogamous, they don't believe in love, they don't have time, they can't find someone intelligent like him.

And one day he realizes that he feels terribly lonely.

And behind all the excuses and all the failed attempts, he has a deep fear of relationships.

Love can be one of the most beautiful parts of life, but it can also be frightening. Having a little apprehension is normal, but some people find the thought of falling in love terrifying.

Symptoms of fear of loving

As we have seen, philophobia is an overwhelming and unreasonable fear of falling in love, which goes far beyond mere apprehension. The phobia is so intense that it interferes in various aspects of one's life.

When the person is about to fall in love, in fact, feels a very intense fear that blocks it.

The normal reaction is to leave as soon as possible, often without giving too many explanations.

This is often associated with fear of intimacy.

The symptoms can vary from person to person and can include both physical and emotional reactions. Here are some of them:

➢ Extreme anxiety and panic at the thought of falling in love or entering into a relationship.
➢ Avoiding places where couples can be found
➢ Excessive sweating
➢ Accelerated heartbeat
➢ Difficulty breathing
➢ Nausea
➢ Tendency to repress one's emotions
➢ Avoidance of other people's weddings or wedding ceremonies
➢ Isolation from the outside world.

Philophobia should be distinguished from social anxiety disorder, although people with a fear of love may also have this disorder. In fact, social phobia causes extreme fear of all social situations, while philophobia is related only to intimate relationships.

If left untreated it can increase the risk of complications among which:

➢ deep social isolation
➢ self-esteem problems

- ➤ depression and anxiety disorders
- ➤ drug and alcohol abuse
- ➤ suicidal thoughts and suicide attempts.

After seeing how this disorder manifests itself, we will talk about the most common causes and then move on to the most effective treatments and strategies to deal with it.

The causes of fear of love

If you want to fully understand the causes of this fear, you need to immerse yourself in the unconscious mind in which we will find the set of ideas you have about yourself, others and the world.

Some of these beliefs may be:

- ➤ love is dangerous
- ➤ I don't need anyone
- ➤ it is better to avoid love because it hurts
- ➤ I do not deserve it

If you were deeply hurt or abandoned as a child, the idea of being able to get close to someone who can do it again is intolerable.

The natural reaction is to avoid relationships, thus avoiding pain. But it is also true that the more you avoid the source of your fear, the more you strengthen it in a real vicious circle.

Bowlby's Attack Theory explains how the mother's ability to tune in to her child is fundamental to her emotional and psychological development. If the mother is unable to respond to her needs or does so ambivalently, it creates enormous damage to her development and her ability to regulate her emotions.

According to this theory, therefore, the fear of falling in love is something we have learned. It is the childhood experiences (as already seen for other disorders) that have laid the foundation for the development of these difficulties.

Of course, in some cases it could just be a recent emotional breakup that keeps you stuck. In this case, you need time to heal.

But if this is a pattern that repeats itself in your life, then childhood experiences are likely to play a major role.

The role of traumatic experiences

If you have had a traumatic experience it is possible that you may develop philophobia: you will try to avoid any kind of commitment, romantic or not, in order not to relive the associated trauma.

Typical experiences are violence, sexual abuse or the loss of a loved one, as well as abandonment and neglect.

Trauma leads the child to defensive behaviors, such as the tendency to hide his true thoughts and feelings and feel always on the alert.

At that time defensive behaviors could in fact help him to survive and were necessary to him. The problem is when they remain in time and lead him to become an adult without contact with his more authentic Self and always on the defensive.

And they prevent him from freely living love and intimacy.

At this point you might ask yourself:

- But I have not experienced a trauma, why am I so afraid of love and relationships?
- Also in this case the Theory of Attack can give us answers.
- The insecure attachment emphasizes that we have not been able to complete important parts of our psychological development.

- These parts are defined as bonding and separation.

The bond occurs when the child develops the feeling of being able to trust others. It should begin at birth and includes being nurtured, supported and encouraged.

Separation, on the other hand, implies that, around the age of 3 years, the child is ready to detach himself physically and emotionally from his mother (or caregiver) with the certainty that the world is a safe place and that he is strong enough to face it.

Without a bond or healthy separation, the child will grow into an adult who will have trouble trusting others to love or care for him.

In this case, so-called "attachment problems" develop.

Other factors in the fear of falling in love

Now let's see what other factors can bring out this disorder:

1. Love makes us feel vulnerable

A new relationship is an unexplored territory and many are afraid of the unknown.

Falling in love, in fact, also means taking a risk. It means putting a great deal of trust in another person and allowing them to influence us emotionally.

And this makes us feel exposed and vulnerable.

Our basic defences are tested. All the habits that we have had for a long time and that allowed us to feel secure and self-sufficient begin to falter.

And we tend to believe that the more we get involved, the more we can hurt ourselves.

2. A new love can reopen wounds of past stories

When we enter into a relationship it is rare that we are fully aware of how we have been influenced by our previous stories.

Our wounds from past stories have a great influence on how we perceive each other and how we decide to behave. This must always be taken into account.

3. Love is linked to a critical inner voice

Many people struggle with the feeling that they do not deserve love. They have difficulty perceiving their worth and believing that someone can really take care of them.

You will surely have noticed the presence of a "critical inner voice" that tells you that you are useless or undeserving of achieving happiness.

This part is formed by the painful experiences of childhood and the critical attitudes we were exposed to at the beginning of our lives.

Although it is there and should be listened to and understood in depth, we must remember that it is only a part, not the totality of ourselves.

4. True joy is followed by true pain

Many people have difficulty enjoying the moments of real joy or pleasure because they think that immediately afterwards there will be a period of deep pain.

And this leads them to move away from what would really make them happy, including love.

5. Love can arouse existential fears.

The more we have, the more we have to lose.

The more a person matters to us, the more we are afraid of losing them.

And this fear can make us more aware of our own mortality: our life has more value and meaning and the thought of losing everything is more frightening.

Now after having seen the symptoms and causes we will now move on to talk about the best treatments and then we will go directly to the practical part.

Philophobia Treatment

But is there a cure?

Treatment options vary depending on the severity of the symptoms. Among the various options are therapy, medication or a combination of the 2.

Psychotherapy

Therapy can help those who suffer from philophobia to face their fears.

It is about identifying and modifying negative thoughts, beliefs and automatic reactions that emerge in reaction to the source of the phobia.

It is also important to examine the source of the fear and explore the underlying pain.

With the therapist's support, you can examine all the relational patterns, trauma and causes that led you to develop this disorder.

Drugs

In some cases, antidepressants or anxiolytics are prescribed, especially if other mental health problems occur. Medications are generally used in combination with therapy.

Face fear of falling in love

The first step is, as always, awareness: to face your fears you must first recognize that you have them.

Obviously, this work of awareness must be addressed to some specific areas.

Review your story

As we saw before when we talked about the causes, to understand what leads us to distance ourselves or defend ourselves from these emotions it is useful to look at our past.

It is not only a question of analyzing our childhood (certainly fundamental) but also of observing our past and present relationships. You could ask yourself some questions such as:

- ➤ What obstacles were there?
- ➤ What didn't work?
- ➤ What kind of problems tend to re-emerge often?
- ➤ How do you move away when the relationship seems to get more serious?
- ➤ What kind of thoughts you have or have had that have led you to drift away?

When we identify the "critical inner voice", we can recognize themes and behaviors and begin to identify so-called recurring patterns.

Recognize real defences that lead us away from emotional intimacy.

If we begin to recognize these patterns, we can trace their roots back to childhood.

In fact, in order to have a satisfactory adult relationship it is often necessary a real break with the relationship patterns of our families of origin.

Stop listening to your critical inner voice

Try to recognize that little voice in your head that feeds you phrases like: "He doesn't really love you. Don't be silly. Leave before it really hurts you".

Think about how this voice teaches you to avoid any kind of intimacy or how it affects your self-esteem with phrases like: "You are too ugly/fat/poor/poor to have a relationship. No one will be really interested in you".

Throughout your life, these thoughts will tend to alienate you from any intimate relationship.

Identifying them will help you to stop seeing them as the only possible reality, but only as a distorted point of view.

Challenge your defences

It is easy to always return to those activities that make us feel safe, to our defences that protect us from the dangers of the world and relationships. But they also make us feel very alone.

Beginning to question and challenge these defences is the first step to change perspective and get closer to the other.

Listen to your emotions

Love deepens our ability to rejoice, passion and emotion.

At the same time it also makes us more sensitive to pain, loss and can resurface previous wounds.

But when we try to avoid pain, we also prevent ourselves from feeling joy and love. When these emotions arise, we should be open to them.

Sadness, as well as anxiety, can be signs of our openness and our willingness to be more vulnerable.

Work on being more open and vulnerable

Being vulnerable, contrary to what is stressed in our society, is a sign of strength.

It means acting in line with the way you really feel.

When you do this, you learn that you can survive even if you are hurt. You will be able to live with more honesty and remember that you are still yourself in spite of everything.

Being vulnerable means being ready to be open to new people and to break old patterns.

Understand that time is needed

It is unthinkable to overcome this problem from one day to the next. You can take small steps challenging yourself every day both to face your fear of love and to be more aware and open.

The fear of falling in love tends to be deeply rooted, so there is no quick solution.

As we have seen, knowing our fear of intimacy and how it affects our behavior is fundamental to having satisfactory long-term relationships.

This fear can sometimes be overwhelming and have a profound impact on our lives, but it is treatable.

It doesn't have to be a prison where we limit ourselves.

Seeking help as soon as possible is the key to dealing with it and starting to live a full and happy life.

CHAPTER 18 • How to Help your Partner if he Suffers from Anxiety

All couples face problems and challenges during their relationship. However, when one of the spouses has been diagnosed with an anxiety disorder, the couple will face a new set of obstacles. The normal problems of everyday life seem to become exaggerated and can strain the relationship significantly.

Living with an anxiety disorder is typically associated with a great deal of personal discomfort, but it can be just as hard on the partners of those diagnosed with the disorder. They may often have to contribute more than normal in financial terms, domestic responsibilities and emotional support.

Financial burdens In relationships where a partner suffers from anxiety, finances can be a major cause of the couple's problems. An anxiety disorder can interfere with the ability to find or maintain employment. It can also limit a person's ability to meet regular monthly expenses. When the entire financial burden of the family is placed on one person (especially if it is necessity rather than choice) discussions and resentments tend to build up and bring excessive stress to the marriage.

Domestic Responsibilities Doing chores, running errands, taking children to school can make you feel overwhelmed. These family activities can take up a considerable amount of time and energy. Keeping the family agenda coordinated requires great attention to detail. When one partner is unable to complete these tasks, the entire responsibility falls to the other. This can contribute to the development of disagreements.

Emotional support

In addition to child and home care, the spouse who does not suffer from anxiety may sometimes take care of their partner or change family activities to ensure that the needs of their anxious spouses are met. People with anxiety disorders often avoid social activities or situations. In this way, their partners' social lives may ultimately suffer, leaving them both isolated and alone. Both partners may feel depressed, afraid or angry.

Help your anxious spouse

Here are some tips to help your partner who has been diagnosed with an anxiety disorder:

- ✓ Know the specific anxiety disorder
- ✓ Encourage and support treatment (individual and couple/family therapy) - Use positive reinforcement for healthy behaviors
- ✓ Do not criticize the irrational fears associated with anxiety
- ✓ Help set specific and realistic objectives
- ✓ Talk about panic, fears, and concerns
- ✓ Be patient and calm
- ✓ Evaluate in a balanced way whether to apply pressure
- ✓ Learn relaxation and anti-stress techniques

Understanding different types of anxiety disorders

There are different types of anxiety disorders. Gathering information about the type of anxiety your spouse suffers from is essential.

Generalized Anxiety Disorder (GAD) is characterized by persistent, excessive and unrealistic concern about everyday things. Social anxiety is the extreme fear of being examined and judged by others in social or performance situations. Even if you recognize that fear is excessive and unreasonable, you are terrified of being humiliated or embarrassed.

Post-traumatic stress disorder (PTSD) occurs in those who have experienced or witnessed a natural disaster, a serious accident, a terrorist attack, the death of a loved one, a war, a violent attack such as rape, or any other life-threatening event.

Obsessive-compulsive disorder (OCD) is a disorder in which individuals experience unwanted and intrusive thoughts that they cannot get out of their heads (obsessions). Often this forces them to repeatedly perform ritualistic and routine behaviors (compulsions) to try to relieve anxiety.

The phobia is a strong and irrational fear. A person with phobias will work hard to avoid certain places, situations or things: animals, insects, germs, heights, thunder, driving, public transportation, flying, elevators, medical or dental care.

5 Things you need to know

1) 1) Anxiety is much more than just a concern. Take it seriously.

Anxiety is thinking too much, caring too much about things and situations, a constant battle between the worst demons in your mind.

Overcoming this mental disorder is not an easy thing. It is not a joke or something that will magically disappear as soon as you wish.

It is for this reason that you have to inform yourself about what your partner is living.

If you do not understand what anxiety is and how this mental health problem affects your partner's health you will not be able to help him/her.

So be willing to learn as much as possible, read, talk to someone who has the same problem, ask for professional help.

Your partner will thank you for the effort.

2) Your partner wants to talk about his feelings. Listen to him

Although anxiety has the power to paralyze the mind and body, your partner will want to communicate with you... if you give him the opportunity to talk.

Listen to what he has to say.

Above all, ask him if he is well and show him that you are willing to offer support and help. Let him know that you are always there for him.

This does not mean that you have to press him and torture him with questions when he panics!

Listen to his needs. Try to understand if he does not want to talk about his feelings. Respect his moments of solitude. He will be grateful to you.

3) His not paying attention to you does not mean that he does not love you. Understand him

People who suffer from anxiety mainly face their inner world. They think a lot, analyze too much, try to win the battle with their worries and fears.

For this reason, they are often absent even when they are physically present.

Your partner loves you and wants to be present; he simply remains a prisoner of his mind and feels powerless in the face of his attempts to stay in touch with reality. Remember this.

He cannot control or simply let go.

Instead of complaining about his lack of attention, hold out your hand and offer him help to show him the beauty of the present moment. Tell him that you know he loves you.

4) Accept and encourage your partner to seek help.

Your partner may have a panic attack. He may have a bad day, and nothing can help him back into the ranks. No matter what you do, it happens.

This can cause worry and frustration.

However, you should not feel guilty. Remain calm. Try to accept the real situation and encourage him to seek professional help.

Your partner knows that you are always there for him, and is grateful to you for staying by his side.

If your partner does not want to face treatment, do not force him or her. Be patient, kind.

Try to find what is comfortable and works well for him.

5) Anxiety can lead to depression. Try to block the first signs

Some researchers associate social anxiety with depression, and if anxiety brings intense emotions and keeps the mind constantly active, depression leads to a reduction in energy and delays everything.

Imagine what would happen if your partner experienced anxiety and depression at the same time! Being torn between two dangers would be a great challenge.

Anxiety and depression generally go hand in hand. Never leave your partner to fight alone. Deal with everything together. Anxiety is a treatable condition.

In addition to this, if you don't think I can get over it alone, don't be ashamed to seek the help of a psychologist, a psychiatrist, a therapist.

Have hope. Believe in it. Remember that your partner is strong, and that you must be too.

CHAPTER 19 • Anxiety in Love

Relational performance anxiety consists of the uncontrollable tendency to try to be accepted, recognized, esteemed and sought after by others. It hides a more innate fear, that of not being up to it.

This particular type of anxiety seems to be characterized by the fear of not deserving the affection of the partner(s), or more generally of significant persons, unless one proves to be capable and skillful.

This underlying belief would prompt people to constantly ask themselves questions that are intended to monitor their own performance, such as: "how should I make the other person happy?", "how should I behave so that the other person does not feel uncomfortable, or rejected?", "how should I do it to avoid being misguided?

All questions that on some occasions it is easy that we asked ourselves, but that someone constantly formulates, in advance of any unpleasant event and behind which are hidden very rigid self-representations that cause a lot of stress and that activate, precisely, a good dose of anxiety.

What does it mean to have rigid self-representations? It means that these people think they can never make a mistake and often, at the slightest actual or alleged mistake, they feel they have done something unsuitable; they get scared and believe they have disappointed their partner's expectations.

They live in an attempt not to make others think badly of themselves.

It's as if by making a mistake they feel they don't deserve a little love, which, in their head, can be achieved only and exclusively on the condition that they make an effort to conquer it, doing the "right thing" and that is, only managing to perfectly meet the expectations of others: a bit like trying to be a "good boy".

In my opinion, very interesting is the strong belief that you cannot receive affection for free, simply because they are what they are, simply because the other person appreciates their presence as it is.

Another detail is that the partner, or the other significant person in question, seems to lose a great deal of will of their own within the relationship. In fact, if we put ourselves in the shoes of the anxious subject, the attitude of the significant person towards us would be determined more by our behavior than by his internal dynamics, his emotions and his way of thinking and living the present relationship.

In short, it is as if they perceive that the fate of the sentimental relationship with the partner is solely in their hands.

This need for control may have developed from a long series of relational disappointments (although probably the causes of this fragility are much older), which were followed by heavy feelings of failure and guilt, fuelled by self-accusations of not having done enough or not having been "good", which in turn reinforced the representation of self as a vulnerable person.

In order to silence these unpleasant feelings, one possibility is to commit to the goal of a constant, and I would even say infinite, attempt to improve oneself: to feel that one can improve oneself in this case means, more than to acknowledge one's need to grow and acquire new skills, to perceive the feeling of not being "enough".

To become "worthy" you need to know how to grasp what to say, do and be in that precise moment; a bit like doing the work of the stopgap: you look for what is missing and try to fill that gap, adapting to the needs of others and the situation ... but very little to your own.

It is therefore clear that being oneself is not enough, but it is necessary to prove that you are worthwhile, that you are always the person that others need and that you know how to get by in any condition.

It is important to be good at everything and you feel the need for the other person to perceive us as indispensable; and this is where something interesting happens in my opinion: the partners move away, maybe even several times, with many pulls and springs, and the reaction is to run after them.

It's a situation that, no matter how much it makes you suffer, is exactly the condition that these people crave. In fact, it is only by perceiving themselves constantly "in crisis" and as never sufficiently "in place" that they can feel immersed in the process of improvement.

Only by choosing a rejecting partner can they find confirmation of their alleged imperfection and find the stimuli to improve themselves more and more. It is a competition in which they constantly hope to exceed their limits and reach the unreachable, which in fact often remains so.

And how could it be otherwise? The goal is not to achieve something pleasant for oneself, because that self is worth nothing.

Alone it deserves nothing, alone that self is fragile and weak and ugly and makes you so angry because it does not represent at all the ideal you want to achieve: complete, armored, strong, brilliant, seductive, able to get by in any situation, to take every opportunity and not let anything slip by, to be able to give everyone exactly what they are looking for. In short, a being impossible not to love.

We said before that it is difficult for these people to recognize, and therefore to remember, the internal states of the affectively close people. A factor that could be associated with this difficulty is the representation of the other as an unreliable person.

Always linked to the numerous sentimental and friendly relational disappointments, the idea that the person at one's side is not really a reliable person may have been reinforced.

It may have seemed to these people that those who had been close to him in the past often did not opt for the best choices, or were not endowed with the best expectations and that these shortcomings led him not to be close to him with the same enthusiasm, or rather with the same concern, that he experienced instead.

The other is a person who is always ready to leave the field, so it is preferable not to inconvenience him and not to rely on him, but rather it is better to take on his part of the responsibility.

To be alert, to be vigilant to notice any change in mood to leave no room for any doubt and no uncertainty, no dissatisfaction is the incessant effort these people make to feel a little safer.

It is better, in fact, to take total control of the situation and risk collapsing defeated taking all the blame.

You can imagine how much weight these people put on themselves and how much anguish they live with in the hope of not finding confirmation to the most terrible of beliefs: not to be worthy of receiving love.

In this suffocating dynamic it is not only the anxious subject who suffers, but also the anxious one, who wants more than anything else to stop him and force him to lower his guard, taking off his armor and appreciating him for free, even with his faults.

In fact, although the partner can be unconsciously chosen for his avoiding characteristics, this trait of his is surely exasperated by the little space that the latter perceives to have.

Feeling the cause of anxiety and sensing that the other is not spontaneous and that he cannot let go, makes his attentions feel cold and detached, as not authentic and in the long run the situation becomes heavy and tiring.

It is difficult for these partners to correspond to the ideals of perfection that the other projects onto them through his pretensions and often end up feeling blocked from expressing any gesture of affection; as if they were experiencing repulsion, as if getting too close means reactivating a circle of stress and anxiety from which it is better to keep a proper distance, which however creates a growing gap and determines the loss of affinity and the pleasure of being together.

Finally, the expectation of finding in the other a safe haven to land when you need emotional recharging deteriorates.

Returning to those who suffer from relational performance anxiety, the loss of contact with a part of oneself is the most important aspect from the therapeutic point of view. Often, in fact, those who find themselves in this situation do not know how to answer the simple question: what do I want?

Too much sucked into the vortex of performance they have never wondered. What do I want for myself? What do I like? What do I want to do? When these people begin to ask themselves such questions, it means that the badly wanted self can be given a chance.

They have realized that they can derive very important clues from it in order to find within themselves the coveted affection and love.

About a month ago I was attending a course of mindfulness in relationship and the teachers had proposed an exercise in which we should contact the loving kindness, the feeling of warmth generated by the interconnection.

I imagined her as a caress on my cheek. However, I realized that it was always my hand giving a caress to someone else's cheek. The enveloping feeling of affection was always something I gave, as if I wanted to play the role of a generous rich man.

That situation gave me the opportunity to reflect on something very important:

what if to donate, to be rich in good things, it was necessary to be willing to receive in the first place?

It is easy to think about this within our relationships, of any kind, as inexhaustible sources of joy and warmth for each other. We would like to be tireless lovers and available friends, children and parents who are attentive, full of love and understanding. We would like to be overflowing with resources, without ever feeling the need to recharge ourselves.

On that occasion I thought I could really give a lot, but only if I gave myself the opportunity to receive, that is, to let the caress rest on my cheek.

It was not a question of pretending, but of allowing myself to stay in touch with what was around me, to remain open to what was coming, and the great discovery was that I felt less need to feel "good" (good partner, good friend, good son etc.).

So it becomes possible to listen to what we receive from every situation and relationship, to feel if we like it, if we don't like it, if it makes us happy, sad, disappointed or hopeful.

We can then feel free to return something according to our current state: do I feel serene and cheerful? Then I will donate all this because I am already receiving it. Do I feel uncomfortable instead? All right, it will mean that I can donate but up to a certain point.

You feel less above everything, beyond anything, less responsible for everything, and you learn to listen to yourself within each micro-moment and ask yourself: how do I feel now?

CHAPTER 20 • The Most Common Errors

Many people fight the problem of anxiety in the wrong way. Alcohol or drug abuse is a great example.

In this way we are not alleviating the problem at all, we are only making it worse.

By using alcohol or psychotropic substances we only inhibit the mind's ability to cope with stress.

As we have said, many people make mistakes with their anxiety, for example, people with panic disorder drink a lot of coffee, making their panic attacks worse.

Others try to breathe faster when they are hyperventilating, because this makes you feel as if you are not taking a full breath, this also makes the situation worse.

But by far the most common mistake people make is getting depressed.

In this case it is called moping, the idea that you need to be alone. The patient believes that to improve their anxiety, just sit down and think.

It is incredibly common, feeling that you need to sit down and do nothing to feel better is one of the main functions of anxiety. You feel like being alone and you lock yourself indoors until the anxiety begins to wane.

Unfortunately, this is a very common mistake that makes anxiety much more powerful. Ideally, you need to stay active. You need to surround yourself with friends and do what you can to get out, exercise and have new experiences. Isolating yourself because of anxiety only makes the problem worse.

The biggest problem is inactivity

Exercise and staying active are not only important for physical health, but for mental health. Movement and exercise improve hormonal function and the production of neurotransmitters, you have to let out excess energy because this could make the body and mind feel more stressful.

So movement and staying active are key aspects of anxiety management. Anxiety changes the way we think, this unfortunately means that thoughts are often our best enemies.

Many people don't realize that anxiety or panic attacks are caused by thinking, so sitting down and thinking could cause the mind to start focusing on negative things.

Staying active, distracting yourself, can greatly reduce the symptoms of anxiety.

Very important is to hang out with people you like and that makes you feel good, this will make your life considerably more enjoyable, surrounding yourself with positive people is a very important tool to fight anxiety.

Finally one of the best strategies to fight anxiety is the definition of your goals, especially because it gives you something to look forward to the future. Staying active with fun activities provides hope, where hope is very important to cure anxiety.

People who become active and distract the mind from negative thoughts are not curing anxiety but just weakening it, curing anxiety is a much more complicated process. However, by the time they face treatment, these people will be more likely to see the results because they will already be in a condition where anxiety can no longer control them completely.

Other errors than anxiety

Errors with respect to anxiety occur almost every day. Anxiety can be very difficult to control, even with the most effective treatment. Common errors of anxiety include:

> - Listening negative / depressed with sad music, rather than cheerful and happy music.
> - Watching horror movies
> - Spending time with negative people
> - Stop using an anxiety reduction strategy just because it doesn't work immediately

The list of errors caused by anxiety is incredibly long, because anxiety causes people to focus on their negative feelings.

Anyway, the first fundamental step is to know what is causing the anxiety, because only in this way we can address the root of the problem.

10 Thoughts that Anxious People Do Every Day

One of the annoying things about anxiety is having to deal with thoughts that get heated and turn into constant worries. Sometimes they are justifiable ("will I have left the oven on?"), but often they are totally unfounded ("Does my boss hate me?"). The brain, however, does not know the difference.

1. Saying something that might offend someone

"Maybe I said it in the wrong way. Trying so hard not to offend that person made it seem even more offensive?"

2. Getting stuck on public transportation

"When a subway train crashes or stops and I don't know the reason for it I go crazy and think about taking a cab, even though I know it will cost me too much and I will take time anyway. I always want to be in control of everything around me".

3. Arriving late

"What time should I leave work to arrive on time? Will there be traffic? Will I find a parking space?"

4. Fear that something might go wrong

"I live in constant fear of what might happen to me and my husband. I am afraid of ending up in the middle of the street and I have no friends or relatives to lean on".

5. Forgetting to do something important

"Every single day when I leave the house, I check that I have locked the door at least 3 times and make sure the refrigerator is locked properly".

6. Not being able to be sure of what is happening or what will happen

"Every day, every minute, I am anxious about what is happening. Something that happened recently or something that could happen in the next few moments".

7. Wondering if your partner is angry with you

"Why is it taking so long to reply to my message? Will he be angry with me? Maybe I'm boring him".

8. Making a mistake at work and thinking that colleagues are judging you

"I made a mistake in the last group email. I immediately corrected it. Now they will think that I am incompetent".

9. Looking stupid in a social context

"Are they laughing at me? I hope I am not wrong. I hope I have not said something wrong. Maybe it wasn't funny? Maybe I wasn't supposed to laugh? Can I leave now?".

10. Be anxious to be anxious

"Many of my anxieties stem from the fact that I am anxious. Why am I anxious? I have no reason to be anxious. I am happy and have a good life. Why can't I get rid of anxiety? Everyone says that anxiety unnecessarily stresses me and I am aware of it. But maybe I make people anxious?".

What happens in the head of the anxious person?

If the person is faced with a situation, it may be a meeting, an examination, a job interview, etc., they will feel anxiety if they exaggerate the difficulties and insist on the consequences of a negative outcome. Anxiety comes from thinking about certain situations: I think about negative things and evoke anxious feelings. At the same time, you underestimate, overlook or minimize your ability to deal successfully with anything scary.

In other words, you give a distorted interpretation of reality that makes you anxious because you imagine dangers that do not exist or that you could deal with efficiently if you were not so incapacitated by yourself, by your anxious reactions.

The anxious reaction is correct, for example: "I am afraid of not passing the exam" It is the thought associated with the situation that is not correct: "I will never pass any exam, I will never be able to graduate, I am incapable....".

The situation gets worse, when the anxious person becomes fully aware of his own unpleasant physical and emotional reactions, he begins to be afraid of them and even more afraid of the situation that triggers them, at that point he will no longer be able to study, entering a vicious circle of emotional and physical suffering that grows more and more intense.

In addition, being attentive to your body increases the messages that our body sends us: if you are afraid of having palpitations, you are constantly listening to your heart and that makes the heart will increase the frequency of beats.

How can I eradicate anxiogenic thoughts?

By identifying these thoughts and then reformulating them realistically, the anxiety itself could be modified and even eradicated.

Let's reformulate the dysfunctional thought mentioned above

"What will happen if I do not pass the exam? My life will have failed before I even start. I feel so bad thinking about it that I can't study. I feel good for nothing, I am useless".

Let's try to identify the trigger that triggers the anxiety

The real and unique fear is that of not passing the exam. The fear can arise from two considerations: having studied little or not having enough confidence in one's mnemonic abilities. In any case, the only way to avoid this concern is to prepare for the exam properly.

Let's reformulate the thought in a realistic way

"I'm afraid I won't pass the exam but I studied. The worst thing that can happen to me is to get a low grade".

Mistakes of thought

When thoughts that cause anxiety occur, you may find that some thought errors fall into these general categories.

When faced with an episode that is an end in itself you have extreme thoughts, for example: I found some hair on the pillow. I am losing all my hair, soon I will be bald".

Catastrophism

Faced with a difficult situation, one imagines a total disaster as a consequence. Example: "I will have to operate on my gallbladder, I will die under the knife".

Generalisation

In the face of a negative experience, such as a lack of promotion, a law will take over the entire existence of a person. Example: "I will never achieve anything in life. I cannot achieve anything".

Distortion

The anxious person underestimates his or her ability to cope with events successfully, forgets all the positive experiences of the past, expects only insurmountable problems and unbearable suffering in the future.

For example, the anxious student will ignore good grades on past exams: he will also forget that this is just one of many exams and that in itself it will not be decisive for his career.

Thoughts of rescue to defeat anxiety

Before dealing with the situation that produces anxiety, we must consider what we can call "relief factors". What should you go looking for? The anxious student can focus on the memory of his good grades, his judicious preparation of many months, the good result of past exams.

To avoid catastrophe, it is better to think of the worst possible consequence of the situation. For example, if the student fails, would this really mean the end of his career? Will he no longer have the opportunity to test his skills? Usually it will be possible to tolerate or "live with" the worst thing. And since the worst thing is unlikely, you will be able to take what comes.

If images of pain or humiliation begin to flood your mind, you will need to make a list and consider each image or fantasy in the light of logic and degree of probability. When you begin to see how illogical or unlikely these images really are, you will learn to deal with them as they come.

If you feel overwhelmed at the thought of actually dealing with a situation that triggers anxiety, you will have to do so gradually.

For example, if a man is anxious and cannot ask a woman out on a date, he can first practice asking a friend. Those who are afraid to climb tall buildings can climb a few floors at a time, first with a friend, then alone. Those who are afraid to leave home can gradually try to get out: first a few meters, then more and more.

When you are already in the middle of a critical situation and anxiety is increasing, it will be appropriate to put into practice the technique of "diversion": focus on various details that have no relation to anxiety. It is not as easy as it seems to focus on something else. Distraction means concentrating carefully on the details. The person who gets distracted should be particularly finicky.

In front of an exam, you will read the brand of a pen or observe the various types of shoes of the various students. In a social situation, the types of fabric, furniture style, people's clothing and fantasies about their lives, interests, etc. will be studied.

Behaviors to Avoid

1. Avoiding situations

If you avoid everything that scares you or that you do not like, you are teaching the little child inside you that it is good and pleasant to avoid all negative things. This is the beginning of the disaster, since in this way you will avoid more and more situations every time just because you do not like them. In the end, you will end up with a mountain of unresolved problems that will cause you great tension.

Avoiding is not always a good strategy to deal with problems. Sometimes, we should simply assume the difficulties and try to overcome them in the best possible way, without complaining about the results.

2. The search for reaffirmation

If every time we face a problem, we have to resort to another person to solve it for us, we will never be able to make a case for ourselves. Seeking reaffirmation can be a good strategy in some cases and undoubtedly makes us feel good, but when it turns into a style with which we face every difficulty it only creates insecurity.

Obviously, when we no longer have a person to console us and reaffirm ourselves, we will feel as if the earth is beneath our feet and we will develop an enormous anxiety. In fact, this is most likely one of the main causes of the high number of suicides that are occurring today.

3. Distraction

We live in the age of distraction, practically everything around us is a distraction from the essence. And we all find it much more comfortable to be distracted than to face our responsibilities. However, if you distract yourself from what is essential you will end up not achieving your goals and this is precisely one of the main causes of anxiety.

If we have set ourselves a goal, we simply have to focus on the path to reach it, avoiding all the distractions that appear along the way. If we sit down at the computer to write an important document, we forget social networks and email; if we have planned to leave your job to start your own business, we forget all the useless proposals that only make us waste time, in short let's dedicate ourselves only to our goal.

4. The permanent control

Many people are anxious because they feel anxious. Now let me explain this pun: it means that they constantly check for symptoms of anxiety and when they find them, they are afraid of them and their consequences. It is a vicious circle in which anxiety generates even more anxiety.

Finally, if you are anxious about a certain situation, you do not necessarily have to find the cause of your state, simply try to change your activity and forget about it. Remember that all those feelings in which our thinking is concentrated tend to become magnified.

Example: tomorrow you have an appointment with a person and this idea causes you anxiety. Now, you don't have to understand why that situation causes you anxiety, but you have to shift your attention.

Do not forget that the unconscious is like a child; if it is not calm, it will never be able to process the concept, on the contrary, it will amplify the anxiety.

It is a mechanism similar to that of physical pain, if we focus on it this will increase; if instead we start a new activity to which we shift our attention, it will decrease.

REMEMBER: any attempt at introspection, at processing the problem should be made when you are more serene or maybe already done.

5. The Importance of Small Things

Many times when we ask ourselves what causes anxiety, we discover that it is those little things to which we give little importance. We worry about many details of everyday life that are not significant but that cause us a lot of tension. If you are one of these people you will have to learn to get over these little things and concentrate on the things that are really important. In this way you will not waste time and energy.

For those who suffer from anxiety, these behaviors will be familiar. However, if you really take this "anxiety diet" and are constant in it, you will experience how the daily tension will slowly disappear.

CHAPTER 21 ● DIY Techniques to calm Anxiety

Jogging

Jogging is more effective than anti-anxiety medications, but without any of the side effects. Studies have compared jogging (and more intense exercise) to drugs and found results that are just as strong, with no risk of side effects.

We have always associated jogging as an activity for physical health care; not everyone knows that jogging immediately offers excellent results for mental health as well. Jogging releases endorphins (mood-enhancing neurotransmitters), relaxes muscles, burns stress hormone (cortisol), improves sleep, and provides mental distractions. The first thing to do then is to run.

Abdominal breathing

If we are affected by anxiety right now, let's observe how we are breathing. It may seem to us that our breathing is too fast and we cannot breathe deeply. This inevitably means hyperventilation, one of the most frequent triggers of anxiety.

So we start breathing better. There is a method of relaxation known as "abdominal breathing" that can be effective, but it can take some time to learn how to practice it. For now, just slow your breathing for a minimum of 15 seconds, taking care to avoid fast breathing or coughing.

This will help us to restore the right balance of carbon dioxide that is lost when over-ventilated. Thanks to this way of breathing we will also restore the right balance of oxygen-carbon dioxide to the brain.

Sensory stimulation

In general, "technology creates more anxiety. Staring at moving lights, like those in nightclubs, watching stressful things on TV, playing with your iPhone - it greatly increases anxiety.

But technology isn't always a bad thing. Anxiety can actually decrease as a result of sensory stimulation. The more we surround ourselves with mental distractions, the less the mind is able to focus on anxiety.... and when we become anxious, the mind is our worst enemy.

The best type of sensory stimulation and doing healthy activities with our friends, such as hiking. But supposing we stay at home and maybe our friends aren't available, we can watch some funny movies, listen to relaxing music, work on a puzzle or talk on the phone with someone we love. These are all effective ways to make thinking about our anxiety much more difficult.

The 2-minute rule

This tool is very effective to solve things immediately. If you find something you need to do, ask yourself if you can do it in 2 minutes. If yes, do it and if it takes longer, ask yourself if it is really important to do it. In this way, you will learn how to solve things immediately and not leave them for the future, avoiding anxiety situations.

Mindfulness

This technique does not refer to a particular state of mind but to a particular type of attitude towards life. Kabat-Zinn defined it as follows: *"mindfulness means paying attention in a particular way; on a goal, in the present moment and without judging"*.

Practicing mindfulness means focusing the focus of your life on the present moment, aware that the past no longer exists, the future is just a fantasy and the only reality available is the perceptual window we have in the present moment, the only moment in which our existence takes place.

"The future depends on what we do in the present. Mahatma Gandhi"

Already following this principle almost all unnecessary concerns are eliminated because most of them are not about real dangers, but are created by thoughts about the past and cause feelings of guilt or regret, or thoughts about hypothetical future scenarios full of dangers and threats and create anxieties and fears.

In this regard it is important to emphasize that in predicting future events the mind will rarely do so in a neutral and impartial way, but for reasons related to the dangerous environmental context in which we have evolved, will prefer scenarios that present various risks and pitfalls. In this regard I suggest you to deepen your knowledge by reading the article "Here and now, learning to live the present".

Anxiety is self-sufficient. Anxiety causes thoughts that increase anxiety

We must make sure that every piece of technology you choose is always focused on happiness and relaxation. Therefore, no dramas, no horror shows, no loud music, no reality TV shows. These activities can relax us, but only on a conscious level. On an unconscious level they stimulate anxiety, and therefore not very effective to promote relaxation.

Restlessness in memory limbo

It can happen to have an anxiety attack without any apparent reason, I say apparent because unfortunately we tend to underestimate the power of our unconscious that records everything that happens to us, including emotions. In practice, the mind has a tendency to feel stress when it focuses on negative things.

For example: the day before we had a fight with our partner and maybe we made peace. This, however, does not mean that the quarrel will not affect the unconscious. In our conscious sphere we have made peace with the monster partner (because we know that our relationship is based on mutual affection) but our unconscious does not have the same ability to synthesize as we do, and as a result it carries the consequences of what was the dynamics of the quarrel.

WHAT TO DO?

We need to intrude on our unconscious, that is, by making a very detailed analysis of what has happened to us in the last 24 hours. Always going back to the example of before, we have to write: "why did we quarrel? Will this quarrel have consequences on our relationship?" "Does my partner still love me at this moment?" "Has the quarrel made me less lovable?" "Has the quarrel made me a bad partner?" "Has the quarrel made me a bad partner? With the answers we will provide to the questions in the case, we must try to calm our unconscious.

Let's start, then, to write down all the thoughts that come to mind, even those that seem more trivial to us. This activity will put those thoughts on paper so that our unconscious will be able to process what we have already processed on a conscious level.

Accepting anxiety

It is also very important to be able to accept anxiety, without always trying to fight it, because, ironically, trying to fight anxiety generates more anxiety, fighting against anxiety is not possible. In this way it is also easier to identify the moments when you suffer from anxiety.

Professional techniques

A very popular technique is EFT; it is based on acupuncture and allows the patient to release emotional tension with small strokes repeated every 6 seconds in different areas of the body.

According to industry experts this technique would bring several advantages: it fights problems such as post-traumatic stress disorders, insomnia, fear, phobias, allergies, panic attacks, anxiety, traumatic memories, lack of concentration, obsessions, depression, sadness, pain, dyslexia, negative memories, nightmares, low self-esteem, obesity, bad self-esteem, etc.

According to experts, it would also prove effective in combating smoking or food addiction.

This technique consists of 14 points related to energy channels (the main meridians of the body) that are used in acupuncture. The points that are worked to treat or alleviate anxiety problems are the beginning of the lashes, the lateral part of the eye (in the bone), under the eye, nose and mouth, the initial part of the collarbone and under the chest.

Many people fight the problem of anxiety in the wrong way

Many people think they are solving the problem or mitigating it, but reality is only making it worse, because strategies are being implemented that unconsciously inhibit the mind's ability to cope with stress. In this regard I refer you to the article "The most common mistakes we make to fight anxiety".

Most people try in every way to manage their anxiety. But why manage anxiety when you can cure it?

CHAPTER 22 • The three Ways to Deal with Conflicts in Relationships

No matter how compatible or deeply in love you and your partner are, sooner or later you will come to some confrontation. A fight is not necessarily a warning sign. When two people live together, it is normal for disagreements to arise. Fights can actually be an essential component in creating an even stronger bond. Therefore, learn to manage the conflicts that may arise between you and your partner and avoid irreparably ruining your relationship.

Keeping Calm and Preparing to Compare

Consider your psychophysical condition. Recovery and self-help groups use the acronym H.A.L.T. ~ Hungry, Angry, Lonely and Tired ~ to indicate a certain malaise that could make people emotionally vulnerable. It is useful to keep this in mind when we are under-resourced and unable to deal effectively with more stressful situations, such as a discussion with your partner.

Sometimes, it is best to address the most basic personal needs before attempting to resolve a couple's conflict. Evaluate your psychophysical condition before trying to communicate with your partner. If you are hungry, angry, lonely or tired, perhaps it is better to postpone the discussion until you have satisfied your needs.

Delay the discussion until you are in control of your emotions. In order to solve problems, you must first take control of your emotions. If you allow anger, frustration or denial to dominate you, you risk altering your judgment and you will come to say or do something you may later regret. When you are in control of your emotions, you may be able to engage in a discussion that is more beneficial to your relationship.

Manage your emotions by regaining calm. If you notice that emotions continue to affect your judgment, you must first master them. Try to regain control using emotional regulation techniques.

For example, you might:

- ✓ Breathe deeply with the 4-7-8 method. Breathe in through your nose counting up to 4. Hold your breath until 7, then let the air out through your mouth until 8.
- ✓ Practice conscious meditation by becoming aware of the body sensations you feel. As you breathe deeply, try to identify what you are feeling and pay attention to the accompanying physical reactions (e.g. closed fists, narrow shoulders, etc.).
- ✓ Call a friend to let off steam or distract yourself from everything that is bothering you.
- ✓ Take your dog for a walk.
- ✓ Listen to relaxing songs.

Make a note of your feelings. The diary is a great tool to relieve stress, understand what you are thinking and collect your thoughts after a fight. You can use it as an emotional adjustment technique or as a way to solve problems, or both.

Get a pen and a notebook and write freely, talking about the difficulties you are experiencing with your partner. Explain in as much detail as possible everything you are thinking, trying and planning to do. By writing down the problem, you will get a better understanding of your point of view and that of the other person.

You can also use the diary to simulate what you would like to say to your partner after a fight. You could start by writing: "My dear friend...". By writing down everything you are feeling, you will be able to clarify your thoughts and decide what to do.

Communicate Effectively

Listen actively. Communication is the key that opens the door to conflict. For it to be effective, both partners need to listen carefully. There are many problems that can arise when you listen to respond rather than understand.

Try these active listening techniques:

- ✓ Eliminate distractions. Turn off the TV and put the phone into silent mode.
- ✓ Stand in front of your partner. Lean in his direction, and look him in the eye.
- ✓ Listen to his point of view before you speak.
- ✓ Repeat what you hear, saying for example, "So, you're saying that ...".
- ✓ Try to put yourself in his shoes looking for a meeting point with his way of interpreting the situation.

Speak in the first person. When the time comes for you to speak, try to express yourself effectively. An excellent combination is to put first-person phrases alongside other statements.

This method allows you to show that you are able to control what you think and feel and avoid putting your partner on the defensive. When a first-person sentence is preceded by other statements, the partner is more likely to focus on the details than we are saying.

For example, you might say, "When you come home and immediately go to bed, I feel like I'm being neglected. This sentence may become more effective if the second part precedes the first: "I have the impression of being neglected when you come home and immediately go to bed.

Focus on the present. Many times a small problem is magnified when one of the two partners begins to bring up past issues. Always try to focus on the present and the problem you are facing.

When you go digging up past issues, it is even harder to deal with them. In this case, one of you can easily say, "Come on, honey, let's not dredge up the past, but try to figure out what we can do now. Is that okay?

Focus on behavior, not on the person. Another possible obstacle to communication arises when one partner attacks the other instead of addressing the problem. If one of you starts a long rant about the other's character, the other may get defensive and nervous.

You highlight a specific behavior such as leaving dirty laundry scattered on the floor, instead of calling your partner "messy" or "sloppy. He will be much more willing to consider it if you do not insult him personally.

Sit next to each other. During a discussion, it is difficult to manage tension without making eye contact. Experts suggest that couples sit next to each other when dealing with particularly sensitive topics.

According to some research, men react better especially when they share certain tasks with their partner, such as housework or walking the dog. Once you are past all the embarrassing and tense preambles, sit across from each other and discuss them face-to-face.

Use your humor. A great way to handle tense arguments is to introduce a note of cheerfulness and light-heartedness. You can resolve a couple's conflict more quickly and ease the tension when one of them makes a few jokes.

Humor should be used at the right time, preferably laughing with the other person and not at her.

According to some research, during a conflict situation it is more useful when humor creates a sense of cohesion - i.e. when making jokes that bring people together.

For example, if your girlfriend prefers to fall asleep with the TV on, try joking about whether she stays tuned to her favorite program while she sleeps. This will help her realize the problem (leave the TV on), without being heavy.

Learn from Fighting to Grow

Respect the differences. Many argue that respect is similar to love because it promotes growth and strengthens bonds. Your relationship will thrive if you make your partner feel respected. Respecting each other's differences means:

- ✓ Show that you realize that his or her opinions, thoughts, ideas and beliefs may be different from yours.
- ✓ To show interest in what he thinks.
- ✓ Give importance to his opinions, even if you do not share them.

Celebrate every time you get through an argument together. Use the fight you are having to make your bond stronger. Think of it as a way to get closer, you will come to accept it.

Once you have thoroughly examined your differences and come to a mutual agreement on a particular issue, do not hold back the outpourings of affection and joy. Be happy that you have overcome your differences.

Look for professional help if the situation is particularly complicated. If you cannot find a compromise or even accept the fact that you disagree with a problem, perhaps it would be wiser to seek advice from a couples therapist.

It may be an alternative if there is a major health problem in your relationship that, left unresolved, would risk feeding disagreements in the long run.

The help of a couple's counselor can give you the appropriate tools to communicate properly and solve the most serious problems that will arise over time.

CHAPTER 23 • How to Remedy

What can you do after a bitter discussion with your girlfriend? You are both likely to feel resentment, anger or confusion. If you want to safeguard your relationship, there is some way to remedy this. Start by analyzing your argument, then try to deal with the situation with understanding and humility.

Analyze the Fight

Try to calm down. You can't expect to settle an argument right after a fight. Since a disagreement has arisen, allow yourself time to cool off your anger. Wait a few hours, or even a few days, to calm down and properly metabolize your emotions. Take a long walk, visit a friend, watch a movie. Try to engage in something that will calm your nerves until you are calm enough to look at the situation more objectively.

Make sure your girlfriend knows you are taking time to calm down. Tell her, for example, "I'm really upset and need time to process the situation. Can we talk about this tomorrow? I would like to calm down now".

Analyze the cause of the argument. We rarely quarrel for no reason. Find time to analyze the factors that triggered the argument and see if you could have acted differently.

Review what happened. Why did you start fighting? What sparked the argument? What did you say to each other? Are you sorry for the words you used?

Keep in mind that memories are subjective, especially in the most stressful situations. It is likely that, unlike you, your girlfriend remembers a certain aspect of the fight. This is normal. It does not necessarily mean that one of you is a liar. It's just that stress can imprint in your memory inaccurate memories, which do not correspond to reality.

Accept what you are feeling. After a discussion, you need to accept and face the emotions that arise. Although we probably hate feelings like anger and sadness, it is important to recognize them rather than ignore them.

By suppressing them, there is a risk that they will implode in the long run. If you feel anger, do not stop yourself from being angry. If you are sad, do not stifle your suffering.

Accept the fact that emotions have not been mental that belong to the sphere of rationality. For example, if your girlfriend hurt your feelings, it is not so useful to realize rationally that she did not intend to behave in a certain way. Keep in mind that both of you are entitled to react emotionally when you disagree, even though your reactions may not be entirely logical and linear.

Porre Rimedio al Litigio

Propose a clarification. When both of you have calmed down, invite her to talk about what happened. After a heated discussion, it is important to find time to clarify the situation with the assurance that both parties have regained the necessary calm to deal with the situation.

Choose the right circumstance to talk so that you do not have external constraints limiting the duration of your meeting. Choose an evening during the week or at the weekend, when none of you are forced to get up early the next day to go to work. Try to address the conversation early in the evening shortly after dinner, otherwise both hunger and drowsiness may interfere with the conversation.

If you do not live together, try to choose a place that is neutral territory for both of you to confront each other. While it may seem strange to you to discuss your relationship in a public place, there is the confidence that in a neutral field you both feel more comfortable. You can find a place frequented by a few people, such as a bar with a spacious and quiet indoor room or a park that is usually not crowded.

Communicate openly with the body. While you talk about your argument, use body language to show you are open to dialogue. In this way the discussion will be relaxed and fruitful.

Look the other person in the eye. Occasionally nod to show that you are listening. Never cross your arms and do not assume postures that make you seem tense. Try to avoid attitudes of nervousness, perhaps playing with your clothes or twisting your hands.

Nod occasionally: this is a non-verbal gesture with which you show you are paying attention to the other person's words.

Use your communication skills well when you speak. While continuing your discussion about the argument you had, use good verbal communication as well. Your girlfriend needs to know that you are willing to find a solution to your problem, so try to express yourself effectively.

Be clear and concise when you speak. Do not include too many details and try to make speeches that get to the point. Do not interrupt your girlfriend when she speaks. Always ask if your words are clear. Ask her for an explanation if you don't understand something she said.

Use first-person sentences. This way you will have the confidence to express your state of mind instead of making judgments about the situation. For example, instead of saying "You overreacted that I was late and you embarrassed me in front of your friends," try "I was embarrassed when you blamed me for being late in front of your friends."

You value the other person's state of mind. It can be very frustrating to hear that your partner does not recognize how you are feeling. Even if you do not agree with your girlfriend about the way she interprets a certain situation, do everything you can to make her understand that you accept how she is feeling.

Often, the simple act of accepting the other person's emotional condition eases the tension that arises in a situation. It can release repressed negative energies and make your girlfriend understand that you are genuinely willing to make her happy.

You may not accept a reaction. For example, suppose she is angry about a joke you made at a party. You might be tempted to tell her, "I was just kidding and now you're overreacting. Even if you think she overreacted, the point is that you hurt her feelings. A reaction dictated by emotion is not something over which you can exert direct control. Instead, try saying to her: "I didn't mean to hurt you, but I am sorry that my joke hurt you. I see how upset you are and I am mortified".

Please note which points you disagree on. In almost all couple problems arise when opinions do not agree. This is normal, because everyone is different. Consider a discussion as an opportunity to understand your differences and how you can find a meeting point.

Perhaps you have slightly different ideas about what a relationship implies. Perhaps you have a different sense of humor. Perhaps you have different needs in terms of time to spend together and moments to devote to yourself. Whatever it is, there are always disagreements in couples about certain aspects of the relationship.

Try to understand if there is an underlying problem that led you to quarrel. If you have a rather heated discussion, it is unlikely that it has arisen from an irrelevant problem. Try to understand what points you disagree on and what you can do to reconcile. Sometimes the simple fact of recognizing that you have a different idea about a particular topic can help ease the tension. If you are able to understand to what extent you differ in character, you will eventually be able to consider some aspects in a less personal way.

Apologize. After thinking about the behavior and the role you played during the fight, apologize for any wrong gestures. Be precise. It is not enough for you to say "I am sorry". Rather, try saying, "I'm sorry I didn't support you when you were studying for your exams. A sincere apology, showing that you listened and understood your girlfriend's concerns, can do a lot to mend the relationship.

Prevent Further Disputes in the Future

Clarify immediately if new problems arise. As soon as you notice a problem brooding under the ashes, do not ignore it. Rather, discuss it before it gets complicated. In this way you will avoid possible outbursts of anger in the future.

If you keep everything inside, you run the risk of regurgitating past things as soon as another argument breaks out. This way your girlfriend will feel attacked and besieged. When a problem arises, deal with it immediately. Although small, it can help fuel resentment over time.

Find a way to resolve arguments without getting angry. Anger can make it difficult to react when the situation gets out of hand. Often you give in to anger and end up alienating those closest to you. Try to find a way together to solve problems without giving in to anger. A good method is to stop for five minutes and express your state of mind instead of trying to talk as soon as a disagreement arises.

Listen to your emotional needs. Often disputes depend on the fact that certain emotional needs are overlooked. When your girlfriend is upset or disappointed in you, try to understand if she has any needs that you are underestimating. Have you moved away from her lately? Have you been so busy that you haven't been able to spend much time with her? Evaluate whether you are respecting her needs and what you can do to make up for them.

Summarize the discussion to make sure you understand. After an argument, always find time to recap what you discussed. How do you feel? How does your girlfriend feel? How are you willing to work to improve the situation and make sure nothing like this happens again? By finding five minutes to focus on the main aspects of an argument, you will prevent it from happening again.

CHAPTER 24 • Communication in Relationship

In order to speak of a couple, there must be two fundamental elements:

- ✓ an emotional bond
- ✓ a shared, future-oriented project.

In today's reality, where the consumerist logic also applies to interpersonal relationships, it is necessary to choose to carry on a relationship with a partner, therefore, it is necessary to want and commit oneself so that this relationship continues over time. Of course, continuity over time must also correspond to a relationship that is healthy and satisfactory for both partners.

A healthy relationship must allow the evolution of the two individuals involved in it and at the same time the evolution of the couple as a whole. It may happen that the structured project initially needs to be renegotiated, either because it has come to an end naturally or because in the meantime the two partners have changed themselves; the objectives that previously seemed to be of primary importance must then be replaced by others that reflect the change and the needs of each.

In life, both positive and negative experiences change people and we cannot pretend to know absolutely, once and for all, the person next to us or assume that he or she is always the same. The human being is in perennial becoming, therefore even his knowledge must assume a character of dynamism, that is, it must continuously change. The other, by definition, is other, different, separate from us, with its own needs that change over time and we must accept it.

Sometimes we try to make him similar to us, but we must keep in mind that it is impossible to cancel differences by making others equal to us: much simpler and more mature, to come to a negotiation, to a resolution of problems that is satisfactory for both, that is, that respects the needs and points of view of each one.

In fact, it is from the acceptance of the other that we have a constructive encounter/confrontation: when I try to adapt the other to me, the dialogue ceases, it is interrupted because it is difficult.

All couples are characterized by three components that are in a delicate balance with each other:

- ✓ sexual
- ✓ emotional
- ✓ social

When one of these spheres is deficient or absent in a constant way, this has a negative effect on the other two that are also debilitated. It may happen that one of these three components compensates, in a transitory way, the other two; if this function lasts over time, the couple in its totality, will enter into a condition of crisis.

The couple will begin its journey towards involution, it will crumble. And when, however, in the face of a situation like the one described, it remains united, this has its psychological cost in terms of signs of discomfort or real symptoms, whose function is to maintain the balance achieved, albeit dysfunctional.

If you want to overcome the crisis and use it as an opportunity for growth, it must be experienced and crossed by both.

<u>What keeps the couple together over time?</u>

- ✓ A sense of "us", a sharing of everything that brings lymph to the emotional bond, a feeling of complicity and psychological intimacy, which are superior to physical passion. We need time and space to spend together.
- ✓ A decisional power equally distributed.
- ✓ A healthy dose of autonomy that allows each individuality to develop and/or continue their passions.
- ✓ The ability to think of being able to live even without the partner, adopting a vision of life aimed at the awareness that everything is transitory.
- ✓ The ability to think that the truth is on one side and the other: everyone has their own reasons and needs.
- ✓ Effective communication

Communication plays an important role in fortifying the couple: dialogue is a capacity that must be nurtured, otherwise it weakens more and more until it ceases, to the detriment of the couple's bond.

Dialogue, in addition to conveying messages, also conveys the way we see the other, for example if we accept it, or if we do not like it; moreover, paradoxically, it must be filled with moments of silence, of listening, where we place ourselves in a receptive perspective towards the other; we create space within ourselves to welcome what the other is really telling us, his answers and his uniqueness that is brought within the bond.

In fact, even silent and respectful listening can help to shorten the distances of hearts.

<u>But what are the contents of this communication?</u>

The exchange of thoughts, moods, ideas, values but also gestures of tenderness and love.

I make myself known to the other when I manifest my feelings, my emotions, my values; in this way the other will recognize me and love me for who I am and how I am. The expression of one's feelings encourages the other to do the same, discovering each other and cancelling the defences.

Obviously at the basis of the willingness to share, there is the desire, the pleasure of getting to know the other and to enter into intimacy with him. Thanks to the exchange, mutual enrichment takes place; we assume that there is always something that others can offer us and something that we can give to others. When this exchange ceases, the individual closes in on himself and the relationship begins its slow agony.

Therefore, deep communication is the one in which the emotions and feelings underlying the events are always made explicit, thus removing those misunderstandings that often happen when we take for granted that it is always the other who has to understand us, even when we are not clear.

Dialogue should not be used as a means to overwhelm, but as a means to listen to the other and understand him, trying to enhance him, accepting him for what he is able to give at that moment: each of us constantly lives situations of tension that are very often "brought into the house" (work, family of origin, friendships, etc.).

Knowing that we are important for the person we love is a source of trust, of security, it pushes us to move forward, to face life with greater strength and not to lock ourselves in ourselves. We all need to be recognized, accepted and confirmed for the qualities we possess.

Moreover, trust in our own problem-solving abilities can make us abandon aggressive and disqualifying tones aimed at humiliating those around us. Anger and aggressiveness show insecurity and inadequacy in managing the situation, while self-knowledge and control of one's negative emotions allow one to see clearly the solution of problems.

According to an American psychologist at Yale University, Robert Sternberg, for a couple to maintain stability over time, three fundamental components are needed that can be placed at the vertices of an equilateral triangle: passion, intimacy and decision/engagement.

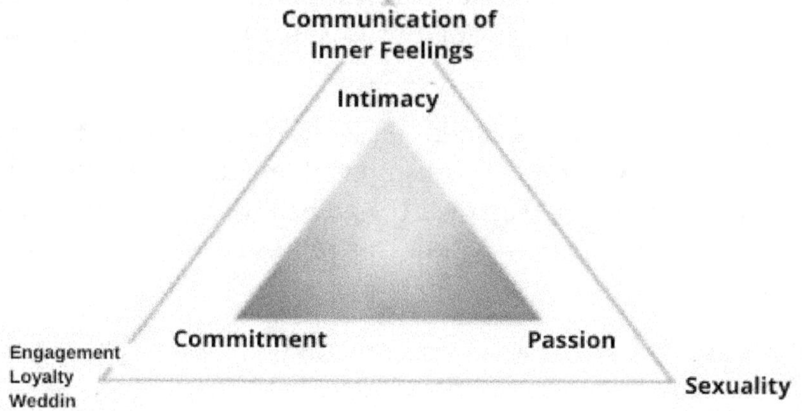

Passion is about sexual understanding. It includes not only "sex", but also the emotional-affective component and that is the set of feelings and emotions of each person: affectivity and sexuality structure each personality, accompany us throughout our lives.

Intimacy concerns the sharing of feelings and thoughts. If we want to know someone but also to make ourselves known, it is important to start revealing ourselves. When you consider the relationship a significant element of your life, an added value in your existence, when there is the desire to be well together, when there is understanding, harmony and mutual esteem, when you receive and give emotional support, then there is intimacy.

The decision/commitment concerns the awareness, choice and decision to start being with a person (short-term aspect) and to want to prolong that relationship (long-term aspect). Sometimes, when you start to love someone, you are not sure that that love lasts forever:

commitment, on the other hand, is what keeps the relationship alive, it is what allows the two partners to evolve together and together to overcome obstacles. This component includes the desire to be with the other, the choice to carry on a relationship over the years, in relation to a shared project. It is a real act of will.

For love to be "forever" it must be accompanied by a conscious intention to spend one's life with the other. Loving someone, therefore, is not only a strong feeling destined, like all feelings, to fade over time, but it is also a commitment that we assume in front of ourselves and the other.

Sternberg's perfect love includes these three components that must be nurtured, otherwise the relationship will fall apart. At different times, one component can prevail over the other, so we can rely on the more solid one or the more solid ones to reinforce the one or the more deficient.

Communication errors in the pair

Couples often make some communication mistakes that they carry around with them for years. They begin as a lack, but end up becoming a habit. These mechanisms prevent you from identifying and solving many of the problems that arise between two people who love each other.

One of the central points in a couple's relationship is communication. The area in which feelings, thoughts and desires are expressed. If you have good communication, everything else comes of its own accord. Conversely, when it becomes ambiguous or deteriorates, new problems may arise in other aspects of the relationship.

The majority of communication errors in the couple occur out of fear or lack of maturity. One cannot perceive the other as a companion, but rather one takes defensive attitudes. For this reason it is always good to make a self-analysis and determine if you are making one of these mistakes. It is important to realize and rectify them in time. Let's see some of them.

Absolutism

Absolutism is a very harmful form of extremism in communication. It concerns an egocentric view of the world and the inability to capture the different nuances of reality. It implies a difficulty in understanding and accepting other perspectives different from one's own.

It is one of the most common communication errors with regard to couples. It translates into a need for total consistency in the other. "If you love me, you cannot cause me any sorrow. As if the human being is not full of paradoxes and contradictions. Absolutism is reflected in the intent to impose conduct. "You must" be like this. You "must" do this or that.

Selectivity

Selectivity occurs when we try to interpret everything through a single category. Unfortunately, this category corresponds to a negative point of view. In other words, everything that characterizes the other is seen in a negative way, even the positive things.

This is one of the most common communication errors in the pair and one that causes the most damage. It is as if there is a need to correct the other all the time, to show him the weakest or wrong aspects of what he does. It characterizes people who are incapable of facing the real conflict.

Extremism

Extremism in communication is similar to absolutism. However, this refers to emotional reactions. Gestures and emotions also form part of the communication in the couple.

In this case, any minor problem becomes a tragedy because of and thanks to this extremist view. Even the most irrelevant difficulties turn into scenes with shouting and crying.

Extremism denotes a lack of self-control and a difficulty of analysis. It is likely that those who exhibit this kind of behavior seek out the father or mother of their childhood in their partner. He wants to show, above all, his childhood characteristics. He seeks understanding and support, as a child would. In the long run, it prevents genuine communication. It does not allow for mutual growth, nor does it promote autonomy.

Anticipation

It is one of the most common errors in couple communication. It happens when one of the two thinks they can predict the other's thoughts. You start with the idea that you know your partner better than anyone else and even think you know their intentions and hidden thoughts.

This type of communication often generates great misunderstandings. It reflects a lack of trust in the partner and paranoia. You always try to interpret and find out what the other person is saying between the lines. It is also an attempt at control.

Labeling

Labeling consists of stereotyping the pair. It is common after a problem or when the partner has made a mistake. From this moment on, it is condemned to remain in a box that defines it. It can be "reckless", "distracted", "irresponsible", or any other. The goal, however, is to mark it with a stamp.

All these are frequent communication errors in a couple. Their most harmful effect is that they undermine the possibility of understanding each other. They affect mutual trust and end up undermining affection.

Communication problems in the couple

One of the most frequent complaints when two partners start a couple therapy is that "He doesn't understand me..." from which all the communication problems originate.

Regardless of the duration of the relationship or the age of the couple, this problem is one of the first signs of a conflict that could become more serious. Very often both would like the other to change. Long conversations, attentive listening and complicity seem a distant memory in their relationship, and have been replaced by apathy, criticism, and a defensive or offensive attitude. Up to the point of selective mutism.

How does communication deteriorate?

During childhood we are guided by the behavior of our parents. When we are teenagers and young adults, on the other hand, attitudes that are typical of our character begin to emerge. Everything we have experienced around us forms a small piece of the puzzle that makes up our world view. But, of course, our partner will have a different and personal puzzle and vision.

In the initial phase of a relationship, the most idealistic one, we form our expectations and fantasies about the other, coming to accept even what we do not like about him. After this phase, however, the first conflicts and often senseless behaviors appear. Here are some examples:

Reading the mind: Typical during an argument. "I know what you are thinking!", "I know you well!". Even if the other did not open his mouth, we believe we can guess his thoughts and behaviors. But how many times have we been wrong in wanting to anticipate the intentions of others?

Indifference: It is a totally irrational way of thinking. It aims to project our thoughts onto the other, just as a lighthouse projects light onto a fixed object.

Minimizing the question: It happens especially when, in moments of tension, one of the two partners would only want to be heard, without judgement, because he feels the need to be understood. Maybe he already knows how to solve the problem, but he looks for a confirmation of his feelings in the partner. Unfortunately, however, the partner often responds only with a: "See, the solution is simple! It wasn't that important".

There are other cases where you respond to discussions in worse ways:

Criticism: There is nothing that can shut you up faster than a "I told you so!". Making comparisons and humiliating the partner creates wounds that make communication impossible, because it is difficult to share one's thoughts with those who believe they know everything.

Escape: It can be physical or symbolic. For example, sitting at the same table and having dinner without crossing each other's eyes or pretending to be busy in front of the TV or with a book as soon as the partner tries to talk to them. This attitude makes both members of the couple feel abandoned and, in some cases, rejected. And so quarrels replace what used to be long, pleasant conversations.

Emptiness, anger, disappointment, frustration, pain and sadness are some of the feelings that awaken in us senseless thoughts. But being silent in front of our partner only increases the pain and feeds our negative thoughts: he doesn't love me anymore, he has someone else, he believes that I am worth nothing anymore... But, sometimes, you will be surprised to discover that it is enough to re-establish good communication to discover that these conclusions were wrong.

The triangle to avoid in the relationship

In a couple's relationship good communication is essential because every wrong step, in the long run, could compromise a marriage or a relationship.

The most common mistakes are usually three and can be represented with a triangle in which each corner has the same degree of importance:

- ✓ Do not listen
- ✓ Assume
- ✓ Wrong approach

DO NOT LISTEN

Anticipate the answers without paying attention to the words spoken by the partner.

As soon as you start to discuss with your partner, show respect and attention for your partner:

Listen to each word to the end without interrupting or overlying it with your voice (even if you disagree). Wait for your moment to speak.

Observe your partner's body language (a frowning expression, lack of eye contact or a low gaze), all those signals useful to understand your partner's mood. There are times when it is best to leave some topics out because you could get devastating results in the conversation.

Manage your body language and facilitate the conversation: nod your head, maintain eye contact. No expressions or "grimaces" that might suggest anything other than a person interested in listening.

PRESUPPORT

Always assume what the partner thinks and wants.

No man has the ability to read the minds of others then:

Explain yourself precisely when you speak. If you think your partner can always understand what you have to say because he has known you for so long, you are out of the way.

Ask questions when you listen, instead of assuming your partner's thoughts and make sure you understand.

Focus on the present and the current problem without reconstructing the facts based on past events.

WRONG APPROACH

Dealing with discussions in the wrong way

When discussing with your partner, consider the following factors:

> Avoid the you! I mean the you that sounds like "pointing the finger" and accusing your partner of an action you didn't like. If you start a sentence with the You, your partner is tempted to get on the defense and will hardly give space to a shared solution. Rather generalize the sentence.
>
> Instead of saying:

"It bothered me today when you raised your voice."

Make the form more indirect (generic) without accusing it:

"It bothers me a lot when people raise their voices."

Admit your responsibilities and apologize. You should honestly acknowledge the positive aspects of your partner and your mistakes if necessary. This way of thinking tells your partner that you are strong enough to admit your mistakes and are ready to build an honest and sincere relationship.

Avoid thinking that there is a "winner" and a "loser" in discussions. You are a couple and as a team you move towards the same goal without winners and losers, only the interest to become stronger together.

Some things to consider when the couple's problem is communication

Many disputes about the lack of dialogue actually depend on the lack of emotional connection.

We are so messed up in our lives that we often put aside relationships to focus on "urgent things" such as completing a work report, doing gymnastics, taking the kids to the gym. If these things are really important, keeping your connection with your partner should be the first of all commitments, as well as walking, making love, cooking and laughing about what happened during the day.

When people say they have communication problems, they are probably talking about how they discuss the problems. Think about it. If you feel emotionally disconnected from your partner and he or she raises an uncomfortable topic, how do you react? In most cases, by avoiding the discussion or putting yourself on the defensive. On the other hand, when you feel close to your partner and important to him, aware of what is going on in your life, and feel the warmth between you, if your partner raises a difficult issue you are more open to listening, right?

The real issue is not what you are discussing.

Even usually in relationships we can list the topics that create tension, it is not really the things we discuss that create disconnection. For example, take a couple where their fights usually follow this pattern: they are both exhausted and too busy, and have not spent time together for days. He is cooking dinner with friends and she forgets the spinach she promised him she would bring.

"You forgot the spinach"-

"Well, if I didn't have to spend half a day running errands for you, maybe I would have remembered," she replies.

And he: "look, you gave me the task of preparing dinner for our friends because you couldn't take care of it, and not only that, you conveniently forget to do the things you said you would do".

How do you think I can continue this conversation? Forgetting that on a Richter scale of importance spinach would be at level 1., this couple is at level 5, or 6 or 7, in a danger zone of insult and anger, because of the way they are talking. When you enter a cycle of aggression, insult and estrangement you stop being on the same team with someone, to become an opponent.

Look below the things you complain about

If you're complaining about something, ask yourself what's under that thing. For example, let's say you realize that your partner is no longer holding your hand when you're around, and this is one of the things you love most in your relationship: that warmth, that physical contact. You find yourself thinking that now you barely touch each other. You could start the conversation by saying, "You're not holding my hand anymore. Realistically, this way you will not get a warm and receptive reaction from your partner, nor will you increase his desire to have physical contact with you.

What is the desire under the complaint? Is that you lack the touch of his hand. "I miss holding hands with you" is a phrase that will most likely get a better reaction than starting with a critical approach.

The problem is never just talking more

In the absence of a genuine connection, talking about stressful topics or seeing you in different positions further burdens communication between two already tired and irritable people. Remember that communication does not always create a connection. Rather, it can create alienation, pain and disconnection.

What brought us together was the feeling of being safe, valued and recognized for who we really are. I've never heard a couple say, "We always find time for ourselves, we have a great sexual understanding, we put each other first, and we have a bad dialogue.

And so remember, the communication that matters most is not the one that happens in words. It has to do with feeling deeply appreciated and valued, which is demonstrated by finding time to be together in ways that do not necessarily involve talking. And when words are important, find words that express to your partner how much you appreciate them, rather than focusing on finding fault.

CHAPTER 25 • The 15 Rules for a Happy and Lasting Relationship

People are often surprised by couples who continue to love each other after decades of marriage. It seems more like a miracle than a great achievement, but it is possible. If you also want to enjoy a long-lasting relationship, you and your partner should follow some common sense advice.

Does finding love only mean finding the right person?

I don't think so.

I believe that finding love means also and above all finding within yourself the strength, will and enthusiasm to build and maintain a balanced, serene and engaging relationship with the person you love.

I am of the opinion that the intensity and depth of a love relationship cannot be evaluated exclusively with reference to the passion and emotions that generally accompany the birth of a love.

On the contrary, if we want to somehow "measure" the quality of a love relationship, it is necessary in my opinion to evaluate the commitment that each of the lovers in the couple puts into building a healthy, attentive, cheerful, positive and, above all, long-lasting relationship.

A healthy, happy and firm relationship represents one of the greatest joys of life.

So, starting today, why not try to take control of the relationship with the person you love?

HERE ARE SOME SIMPLE RULES TO SUCCEED:

1) <u>In love with those who have love to give you</u>

It is a golden rule, which is why it deserves first place. Do not think that a person falls in love with time, especially if too much time! Even more so, especially if they are married or already in love with another person or too much in love with themselves. Do not chase relentlessly a person who gives you love with the eyedropper. This attitude is typical of those who have unresolved problems of emotional addiction, low self-esteem and many others.

2) <u>Look for a partner among the people you share something with.</u>

Do opposites attract each other? Maybe so, but this attraction may be too short because the possibilities of being together are exhausted by intellectual and emotional incompatibilities. When the basic differences between two people are few, their chances of colliding are also greatly reduced. The key words of this commandment are: complicity and sharing.

3) <u>Observe. Do not imagine and above all do not project</u>

It happens too often, at the beginning of a relationship, many people convince themselves that they have met the man or woman in their life. When we fall in love, we all tend to project and idealize and so we attribute qualities to the candidate that he does not have, but that we would like him to have. The secret is: not to create false expectations and not to see things that are not there.

4) <u>Do not get bored</u>

Having common interests helps a lot to win the test of boredom that usually occurs when the relationship is down at an advanced stage.

5) <u>Set the rules before starting a relationship</u>

Many people lie or hide the truth at the beginning of a relationship with the hope of impressing or pleasing the other more. Don't get me wrong, this doesn't mean abolishing niceties, attention is perfect but not if they flaunt falsehoods about you. For example, if you hate soccer and do not like to wear miniskirts, to please him do not buy two tickets to the stadium and make it clear that you prefer pants! You have to show your expectations right away so he won't disappoint you and he won't expect something from you that you can't/will not give him.

6) <u>If he did it to her, he can do it to you too.</u>

This commandment should deserve first place instead we find it only in the sixth because we are all incurable romantics and therefore, we think that "for love can change".

The truth is that if a person cannot be proud of his sentimental conduct, you have to be careful, what he did to his ex (to his ex!) can do it to you too, maybe in a different way or maybe not immediately, but he could do it again.

It is always better to pay attention, both to how he has behaved in past experiences and to how he relates in the present to the people around him. In this way you will have the tools to react and take measures as soon as you notice a particular attitude of your partner that you do not like. It's raw and it's awful but if he left his ex-abruptly to "run away" with you, he might as well leave you for someone else in a similar way. Commandment number six is not meant to generalize just to invite you to take a closer look.

7) <u>Don't sacrifice yourself</u>

Never give up something that is important to you to get his affection or worse, to please him. Don't give up your job, don't neglect friendships or family relationships. Don't do without your political ideas or beliefs either. Never lose something of yourself, never give up emotional ground in exchange for affection: if you start to give up a part of you, of your personality, what you will live will no longer be a healthy relationship.

8) <u>Equal relationship</u>

Do not build a report on the foundations of blind admiration. If you start thinking "I don't deserve it", or "it's too good for me", then things aren't going well, it could be that you're starting to develop some kind of emotional addiction. A healthy relationship is either PARTICIPAL or not at all.

9) <u>Don't have secrets</u>

Don't say you love children if you don't want to have children, don't lie about how much you earn and so on. You need to be able to confide in your partner, you need a companion to support you and you don't have to feel the need to hide from him. Establishing true intimacy is risky but also exciting and rewarding. Being able to find support and trust in each other is the most radiant promise of happiness in a relationship.

10) <u>You deserve to be happy</u>

Don't fall into concepts like "My life without you doesn't make sense" or even worse, "I can't live without you". A healthy person will be able to tell you "I don't want to live without you": a relationship should never be based on addiction or suffering. Set yourself the goal of being happy and if by chance you think you are different and do not deserve happiness, you are making a big mistake and you should care more about your self-esteem.

11) <u>Do not make comparisons</u>

People don't fall in love with what makes you exactly the same as others, but with what makes you different, unique in your qualities and flaws.

Be yourself as you are, imperfectly perfect.

We are not perfect for everyone; we are perfect only for that small circle of people who really take the time to get to know us and love us for who we really are.

So don't make the mistake of comparing your relationship with your partner with other relationships: neither with your parents or your friends, nor with that couple you know superficially and whose relationship seems perfect.

Each couple has its own rules, mechanisms and balances.

Don't worry about comparing your relationship to others: focus on your own and make it special and wonderful.

12) <u>Listen without judgment and resolve contrasts with serenity</u>

It's all too easy to look at someone superficially and make a hasty and equally superficial judgment.

Instead, try to give yourself time to really get to know each other.

What a person shows to the public is just a small fraction of an iceberg hidden deep inside.

And most of the time, this iceberg is furrowed by cracks and scars that run all the way to the center of their person.

Never judge. Learn to respect and recognize your partner's feelings.

Pay attention to them.

Try to be always present.

We do not always need advice.

Sometimes all we need is a hug, an ear that listens and a heart that understands us.

Fighting is almost always just a waste of time and energy.

The quarrel is a wasted opportunity to spend a pleasant moment of serenity.

In the same way, sterile quarrels get you nowhere and have only the consequence of feeding resentments and quarrels.

If an aspect of your relationship with your sweetheart upsets you, calmly manifest to your partner the need to deal with the topic and express your thoughts in a gentle and calm way.

This is the best way to resolve contrasts and friction.

Don't become rigid in your position and don't give up taking a step backwards: this doesn't mean that you are not asserting your reasons, but simply that you have understood that the happiness of your relationship is more important than your need to be right.

13) <u>Share what you feel in your heart</u>

Share what is happening in your mind and heart.

Share your deepest thoughts, needs, desires, hopes, dreams and fears.

Open communication and complete honesty are vital for a healthy relationship.

Transmit your thoughts and emotions to your partner, don't expect or wait for him to know them if you don't tell him about them.

Information is what keeps communication fluid and fully functioning.

So, start communicating clearly.

Don't try to read other people's minds, and above all, don't wait for others to interpret the thoughts you don't express.

14) <u>Support each other in hard times.</u>

Make sure you are always there, both in good times and bad.

Celebrate his or her victories with your partner and offer him or her comfort when he or she fails.

Be ready to support him in all circumstances, make sure he never feels abandoned.

Both of you should be certain that you can trust each other, not only in moments of happiness, but especially when everything else seems lost.

Value the time you spend together.

As a couple, take time for each other.

With our many commitments we often forget to relax and enjoy the beautiful relationship we have built.

So always try to make sure you dedicate quality time to the person you love.

Regardless of distance and distance, make your partner feel that you are there, that you are present, attentive to his needs and requirements.

Cut out special moments just for you two at least once a week.

Do something fun.

Spend time together talking, taking walks, chatting and laughing in a carefree way.

Get away from the problems and thoughts of everyday life and make sure you are totally present for the other person.

Don't miss any opportunity to openly appreciate what you like most about your partner.

Just because you are a couple, do not think that those qualities are your acquired right, to be taken for granted.

Praise then your sweetheart, share her successes and joys, emphasize her merits and strengths.

Support her progress and rejoice at her victories, encouraging her goals, dreams and ambitions.

15) <u>Love and respect yourself first and foremost</u>

Our first and last love is first and foremost love for ourselves.

Do not rely on your partner or anyone else to achieve your happiness and self-esteem.

You alone are responsible for this.

If you are not the first to love yourself, why should someone else?

Love the person you are, for better or for worse, and never stop trying to improve yourself.

Live your life with passion, intensity and enthusiasm, making the changes you think are necessary not to please others, but because in line with what you think is right.

CONCLUSION

Thank you for coming all the way to the end of this book, we hope it was informative and able to provide you with all the tools you need to achieve your goals, whatever they may be.

This book has tried to bring all the important points to the fore so that you can get all the benefits to overcome anxiety in relationships without having to deal with the negative effects.

All you have to do is follow the information provided in the book and follow the directions.

I hope this book really helps you to overcome the difficulties and achieve your goals.

Finally, if you have found this book useful in any way, a review on Amazon is always appreciated!